THE ADOPTION INCENTIVES PROGRAM

BACKGROUND AND FUNDING

SOCIAL ISSUES, JUSTICE AND STATUS

Additional books in this series can be found on Nova's website
under the Series tab.

Additional E-books in this series can be found on Nova's website
under the E-book tab.

SOCIAL ISSUES, JUSTICE AND STATUS

THE ADOPTION INCENTIVES PROGRAM

BACKGROUND AND FUNDING

PATRICK L. CALES
EDITOR

New York

For permission to use material from this book please contact us:
Telephone 631-231-7269; Fax 631-231-8175
Web Site: http://www.novapublishers.com

NOTICE TO THE READER

The Publisher has taken reasonable care in the preparation of this book, but makes no expressed or implied warranty of any kind and assumes no responsibility for any errors or omissions. No liability is assumed for incidental or consequential damages in connection with or arising out of information contained in this book. The Publisher shall not be liable for any special, consequential, or exemplary damages resulting, in whole or in part, from the readers' use of, or reliance upon, this material. Any parts of this book based on government reports are so indicated and copyright is claimed for those parts to the extent applicable to compilations of such works.

Independent verification should be sought for any data, advice or recommendations contained in this book. In addition, no responsibility is assumed by the publisher for any injury and/or damage to persons or property arising from any methods, products, instructions, ideas or otherwise contained in this publication.

This publication is designed to provide accurate and authoritative information with regard to the subject matter covered herein. It is sold with the clear understanding that the Publisher is not engaged in rendering legal or any other professional services. If legal or any other expert assistance is required, the services of a competent person should be sought. FROM A DECLARATION OF PARTICIPANTS JOINTLY ADOPTED BY A COMMITTEE OF THE AMERICAN BAR ASSOCIATION AND A COMMITTEE OF PUBLISHERS.

Additional color graphics may be available in the e-book version of this book.

Library of Congress Cataloging-in-Publication Data

ISBN: 978-1-62948-758-8

Published by Nova Science Publishers, Inc. † New York

CONTENTS

PREFACE

This book discusses background related to the Adoption Incentives program, including the longstanding Congressional interest in domestic adoption and the significant increases in adoptions from foster care that have occurred since the middle 1990s. It also discusses the current program, including the incentive structure.

Chapter 1 – Under the Adoption Incentives program (Section 473A of the Social Security Act) states earn federal bonuses when they increase adoptions of children who are in need of new permanent families. All 50 states, the District of Columbia, and Puerto Rico have earned a part of the $375 million in Adoption Incentive funds that have been awarded since the program was established as part of the Adoption and Safe Families Act of 1997 (ASFA, P.L. 105-89). Funding authorized for this program has been extended twice since it was established, most recently in 2008 (P.L. 110- 351), but is currently set to expire on September 30, 2013. Congress may act to revise and/or extend this program in the 113th Congress.

Congress has long shown interest in improving the chances of adoption for children who cannot return to their parents and who might otherwise spend their childhoods in temporary foster homes before "aging out" of foster care. Since ASFA's enactment in 1997, the annual number of children leaving foster care for adoption has risen from roughly 30,000 to more than 50,000 and the average length of time it took states to complete the adoption of a child from foster care declined by close to one year (from about four years to less than three). Over the same time period, and in significant measure due to the greater number of children leaving foster care for adoption and at a faster pace, the overall number of children who remain in foster care declined by 29%— from a peak of 567,000 in FY1999 to 401,000 in FY2011. Despite these successes, however, the number of children "waiting for adoption" (104,000 on the last day of FY2011) remains more than double the number of children who are adopted during a given year. Adoptions of older children remain far less common than adoptions of younger children, and some 26,000 youth aged out of foster care in FY2011, compared to just 19,000 in FY1999.

Chapter 2 – This is Testimony of Nicole Dobbins, Executive Director, Voice for Adoption. Hearing on "Increasing Adoptions from Foster Care."

Chapter 3 – This is Testimony of Rita L. Soronen, President and CEO, Dave Thomas Foundation for Adoption. Hearing on "Increasing Adoptions from Foster Care."

Chapter 4 – This is Testimony of Kelly Rosati, Vice President of Community Outreach, Focus on the Family. Hearing on "Increasing Adoptions from Foster Care."

Chapter 5 – This is Testimony of Pat O'Brien, Executive Director, You Gotta Believe! The Older Child Adoption & Permanency Movement, Inc. Hearing on "Increasing Adoptions from Foster Care."

In: The Adoption Incentives Program   ISBN: 978-1-62948-758-8
Editors: Patrick L. Cales   © 2014 Nova Science Publishers, Inc.

Chapter 1

CHILD WELFARE: STRUCTURE AND FUNDING OF THE ADOPTION INCENTIVES PROGRAM ALONG WITH REAUTHORIZATION ISSUES*

Emilie Stoltzfus

SUMMARY

Under the Adoption Incentives program (Section 473A of the Social Security Act) states earn federal bonuses when they increase adoptions of children who are in need of new permanent families. All 50 states, the District of Columbia, and Puerto Rico have earned a part of the $375 million in Adoption Incentive funds that have been awarded since the program was established as part of the Adoption and Safe Families Act of 1997 (ASFA, P.L. 105-89). Funding authorized for this program has been extended twice since it was established, most recently in 2008 (P.L. 110-351), but is currently set to expire on September 30, 2013. Congress may act to revise and/or extend this program in the 113th Congress.

Congress has long shown interest in improving the chances of adoption for children who cannot return to their parents and who might otherwise spend their childhoods in temporary foster homes before "aging out" of foster care. Since ASFA's enactment in 1997, the annual

---

* This is an edited, reformatted and augmented version of Congressional Research Service, Publication No. R43025, dated April 18, 2013.

number of children leaving foster care for adoption has risen from roughly 30,000 to more than 50,000 and the average length of time it took states to complete the adoption of a child from foster care declined by close to one year (from about four years to less than three). Over the same time period, and in significant measure due to the greater number of children leaving foster care for adoption and at a faster pace, the overall number of children who remain in foster care declined by 29%—from a peak of 567,000 in FY1999 to 401,000 in FY2011. Despite these successes, however, the number of children "waiting for adoption" (104,000 on the last day of FY2011) remains more than double the number of children who are adopted during a given year. Adoptions of older children remain far less common than adoptions of younger children, and some 26,000 youth aged out of foster care in FY2011, compared to just 19,000 in FY1999.

Under the current Adoption Incentive bonus structure, states earn $4,000 for each adoption of a foster child that is above the number of foster child adoptions finalized by the state in FY2007 and $8,000 for each adoption of an older child (9 years or older) above the number of older child adoptions it finalized in FY2007. If a state has earned an award in either of those categories—or if it improves its adoption rate—it earns $4,000 for each adoption of a special needs child (under age 9) that is above the number of such adoptions it finalized in FY2007. For improving its rate of adoption (above the rate it achieved in FY2002 or a later year with a higher rate), a state is eligible for additional incentive funds of $1,000 multiplied by the increased number of adoptions that are calculated to have resulted from the improved adoption rate. However, increases in incentive amounts states earn due to improved adoption rates are only paid to those states if sufficient program appropriations are available after all awards for increases in the number of adoptions have been made.

In the four years (FY2008-FY2011) that the *current* incentive structure has been in place, states were eligible for incentive payments of $166 million. Of that amount, states earned $74 million for increases in the number of foster child adoptions, $45 million for increases in older child adoptions, and $37 million for increases in special needs (under age 9) adoptions, and they were eligible for increases of $10 million in their incentive payments for improvements in their rates of adoption. However, most appropriations provided for the Adoption Incentives program were needed to pay awards for the increased number of adoptions, and states received less than $2 million of the incentives for which they were eligible due to improved rates. Therefore, states are expected to receive no more than $158 million of the $166 million of the bonus funds for which they were eligible for adoptions finalized in FY2008-FY2011.

States are permitted to use Adoption Incentive bonuses to support a broad range of child welfare services to children and families. Many states report spending incentive funds on adoption-related child welfare purposes, including post-adoption support services, recruitment of adoptive homes, and training or conferences to improve adoption casework. A smaller number of states report using these funds for adoption assistance payments, improved adoption homes studies, child protection casework, foster care maintenance payments, or other child welfare purposes.

Funding for the Adoption Incentives program is provided on a discretionary basis as part of the annual appropriations process. The program is authorized to receive $43 million annually (through FY2013), but in recent years actual appropriations have been around $39 million. Final FY2013 appropriations for the Adoption Incentives program were included in the Consolidated and Further Continuing Appropriations Act, 2013 (P.L. 113-6) at this same level. However, those appropriations are subject to a 5% reduction (under the March 1 sequestration order).

At a February 27, 2013, hearing of the House Ways and Means Subcommittee on Human Resources, witnesses called for reauthorization of the Adoption Incentives program and especially stressed the need to find and support permanent families for older youth and other harder to place youth.

As part of its FY2014 budget request, the Administration calls for reauthorization of the program and proposes requiring states to spend their Adoption Incentive funds on "trauma-informed services to improve social and emotional well-being of children waiting for adoption or those having achieved adoption." The Administration does not propose other changes to the program and it seeks FY2014 funding for Adoption Incentives at the same level that was provided in FY2012 ($39 million).

INTRODUCTION

The Adoption Incentives program (Section 473A of the Social Security Act) provides federal bonus funds to state child welfare agencies that increase adoptions of children who are in need of new permanent families. Generally, these are children for whom reuniting with their biological parents is not possible and who would otherwise be expected to remain in public foster care until they "age out" (that is, reach the state age of majority or the age at which state custody of children in foster care is ended). The first awards under the program were made to states (in FY1999) for improvements in numbers of adoptions in FY1998 and the most recent were made (in FY2012) for improvements in numbers of adoptions in FY2011. Through FY2012, more than $375 million in bonus funds have been awarded under the Adoption

Incentives program. Currently states are eligible to receive these incentives for increases in adoptions finalized through FY2012 and funding to pay those bonuses is authorized through FY2013.

The 113th Congress will likely consider whether to extend the Adoption Incentives program. This report discusses background related to this program, including the longstanding Congressional interest in domestic adoption and the significant increases in adoptions from foster care that have occurred since the middle 1990s. It discusses the current program, including the incentive structure. State child welfare agencies may receive separate bonuses for increases in the number of adoptions of (1) foster children, (2) older children (9 years or older), and (3) children under age 9 who are determined to have "special needs." In addition, they may be eligible for increases in their incentive awards for an improved rate of adoption. The report also includes a discussion of some issues Congress may consider as part of the reauthorization debate and it notes reauthorization-related activities.

Throughout this report some unique terms related to adoption, foster child adoptions, or the Adoption Incentives program are used, e.g., "special needs" and "adoption rate." While each of these terms is explained in the body of the report, for ease of reference, they are also included in a "Glossary of Terms" provided in Appendix A to this report.

Congressional Interest in Adoptions from Foster Care

Foster care is a temporary living arrangement for children for whom remaining in their own homes is not safe or appropriate. Most children who enter foster care are ultimately reunited with their parents. However, when reunification is determined not possible or appropriate, adoption is generally considered the best way to achieve a new permanent family for a child.

Congress has long shown an interest in encouraging adoptions of children who would otherwise remain in foster care until they age out. In 1978, the Adoption Opportunities program (Title II of the Child Abuse Prevention and Treatment and Adoption Reform Act, P.L. 95-266) was enacted to require federal administrative coordination of adoption and foster care programs and to support research and other activities to "facilitate elimination of barriers to adoption and to provide permanent and loving home environments for children who would benefit from adoption, particularly children with special needs." In 1980, Congress enacted the Adoption Assistance and Child Welfare Act (P.L. 96-272), including the first federal support for ongoing subsidies to eligible adoptees with "special needs" (under a new Title IV-E of the Social Security Act). In this context the "special needs" designation applies to children in need of new permanent families (i.e., they cannot be returned to their parents) and who have conditions or factors that makes it harder to find them adoptive homes without offering assistance. States may establish their own factors to determine special needs, but commonly use factors such as a child's older age; membership in a sibling group; medical condition; mental, physical or emotional disability; or membership in a minority race/ethnicity.[1]

By 1997, a renewed concern about the failure to move children from foster care to permanent families was an important impetus for the Adoption and Safe Families Act (ASFA, P.L. 105-89). As part of that law, Congress made changes to federal child welfare policy that were intended to ensure that states focused on achieving expeditious permanence for children in foster care, including through adoptions whenever appropriate. Among other changes, the law tightened or added new permanency planning timelines for children in foster care, required states to spend certain federal child welfare funds (under the Promoting Safe and Stable Families Program) for adoption promotion and support services, and authorized financial bonuses to states that increase adoptions of children out of foster care under the newly created Adoption Incentives program.[2,3]

Adoptions with Public Child Welfare Agency Involvement

Adoption is a social and legal process by which a child gains a new and permanent family. For each child in foster care who cannot be reunited with his or her parents and for whom adoption is determined to be the child's route to permanency, the state must identify suitable and willing adoptive parent(s). States may begin the process of recruiting an adoptive family before a child is "legally free" for adoption. However, before the child's adoption may be finalized a state (or tribal) court must generally terminate any existing parental rights or responsibilities to a child. Once this process, referred to as "TPR" (for termination of parental rights), has been completed, the child's adoption by new parents may be finalized by a state or tribal court.[4]

Since the 1997 enactment of ASFA, the annual number of adoptions out of foster care rose significantly and the rate of adoptions has doubled. There are fewer children in foster care who are "waiting for adoption," and the average time it takes to complete an adoption has declined by roughly one year. At the same time, the number of children waiting for adoption remains more than double the number of those adopted each year and adoptions of older children remain less common than those of younger children.

Growth in the Number of Adoptions out of Foster Care

The annual number of adoptions from foster care climbed from less than 30,000 in the mid- 1990s, to a peak of some 57,000 in FY2009. Since then (through FY2011) the number has remained at, or above, roughly 50,000. The rise in the number of adoptions played a significant role in the decline in the overall number of children in foster care, which peaked in FY1999 at 567,000 children and had declined by 29%, to 401,000 children, as of the last day of FY2011.[5]

The fact that the number of foster child adoptions has remained relatively high, despite the decline in the overall number of children in foster care, is notable. Viewed as a rate—that is the number of children adopted during a given fiscal year for every 100 children who were in foster care on the last day of the preceding fiscal year—public child welfare agency adoptions doubled since the late 1990s (from a rate of roughly 6 adoptions per 100 children in foster care to 12 per 100). (See Table B-1 in Appendix B for annual data on number and rate of adoptions.)

Decline in Children in Foster Care Waiting for Adoption

For roughly one-quarter of the children in foster care on a given day, adoption has been identified as their case plan goal—that is, their exit strategy to permanency.[6] Some children with a permanency goal of adoption, and certain other children in foster care, are "legally free" for adoption—meaning the rights of both parents have been terminated. These children—those with a case plan goal of adoption and/or for whom all parental rights have been terminated are generally referred to as children who are "waiting for adoption." [7]

For most of FY1998-FY2011, the number of children waiting for adoption was between 130,000 and 135,000. However, in recent years this number has declined and it stood at 104,000 as of the last day of FY2011. Additionally, the share of waiting children who leave foster care for adoption generally grew across this time period. Specifically, the number of children adopted from foster care in FY1999 was 37% of all children waiting for adoption on the last day of FY1998; the comparable percentage for children adopted in FY2011 was 46%. (See Table B-2 in Appendix B for annual data on the number of waiting children and the share adopted in the following year.)

Even though the number of waiting children has declined, that number represents a slightly larger share of the overall foster care caseload in FY2011 (26%) than was the case in FY1998 (22%). This relatively modest increase in share of children in foster care waiting for adoption—coinciding with greater success in moving waiting children to adoption—might reflect changes in state practice regarding who may be assigned a case goal of adoption. Alternatively, or in addition, it might be the result of state efforts to reduce unnecessary entries to foster care—which in turn could mean a higher percentage of those entering will need to find a new permanent family via adoption.

Reduced Time to Adoption

Adoption is a multi-step legal and social process that takes time to accomplish. Children who enter foster care do not typically move directly to adoption. With limited exceptions federal policy requires that a state must make "reasonable efforts" to reunite a child with his or her family.[8] When reunification is determined not possible however, the state must take certain steps to free a child for adoption. Specifically, as amended by ASFA, federal law requires a state to petition a state court for termination of parental rights (TPR) to the child if a state court finds either that the child is an abandoned infant (as defined in state law) or that reasonable efforts to reunite the child and his/her parents are not required (because the parent has committed one of certain heinous crimes against the child or his/her sibling). Additionally, once a child has been in foster care for 15 out of the last 22 months, the state must petition the court for TPR, unless it can document for the court that doing so would not be in the child's best interest, that services necessary for reunification and agreed to in the child's case plan have not been provided, or that the child is living with a relative.[9] The state court must then determine—based on state laws defining when parental rights may be severed—whether to grant TPR.[10] At the same time, for any child who cannot be reunited and whose case plan goal is adoption, the state agency must work to find an appropriate and willing adoptive family. Once this step is complete, and a child is successfully placed with the family, a state court must again act, this time to finalize the adoption and, as part of this process, to formally provide the adoptive parents with all legal parental rights and responsibilities for the child.

Since FY2000, the amount of time a child spends in foster care before leaving via a finalized adoption has declined by roughly one year. Most of this reduction in time is a result of the shorter time frame needed to reach TPR. However, there has also been some decline in the amount of time it takes to finalize a child's adoption after TPR is completed. On average, adoptions of children out of foster care that were finalized in FY2000 took just under four years to complete (45.9 months). By contrast, children who reached a finalized adoption in FY2011 did so, on average, in just under three years (34.0 months). (For annual data on average and median time from removal to finalized adoption see Table B-3 in Appendix B.)

ADOPTION INCENTIVES

Promoting the use of adoptions to ensure children who would otherwise remain in foster care have a permanent family has been a driving purpose of the Adoption Incentives program since its creation. The program has also sought to provide special incentives to states for adoptions of children who are considered harder to place in adoptive homes, including children with special needs and older children.[11] Established by ASFA in 1997 (at Section 473A of the Social Security Act) the Adoption Incentives program has been amended and extended twice: first, by the Adoption Promotion Act of 2003 (P.L. 108-145), and, more recently, by the Fostering Connections to Success and Increasing Adoptions Act of 2008 (P.L. 110-351).

Each reauthorization of Adoption Incentives has made some changes to the incentive structure used to determine awards, including the categories for which awards may be earned, the "baselines" used to determine improvement, and/or the amount of the individual incentive awards. The current incentive structure is described below. (Appendix C includes a table that shows development of the incentive structure across program reauthorizations.)

How Do States Earn Incentive Funds?

States may earn Adoption Incentive funds in four ways. For an increase in the

- number of children adopted out of foster care overall;
- number of children adopted at age 9 or older;
- number of children adopted with special needs and who are under the age of 9; or
- rate at which children are adopted from foster care.

Whether a specific state has increased the *number* of adoptions is determined by comparing the number of adoptions that the state finalized during the fiscal year to the number of such adoptions it finalized in FY2007 (the "baseline" year). A state is determined to have increased its *rate* of adoption if the percentage of children adopted from foster care (as a share of the number of all children in foster care in the prior year) is greater than it was in FY2002, or in any succeeding fiscal year prior to the year for which the award is being determined.

Amount of Incentives

An eligible state earns $4,000 for each foster child adopted above its baseline number of foster child adoptions and $8,000 for each older child (age 9 or above) adoption above its older child adoption baseline.[12] If a state has earned an award in either of those categories—or if it improves its adoption rate—it also earns $4,000 for each adoption of a special needs child (under age 9) that is above its baseline number of such adoptions. Finally, for an improvement in its rate of adoption, a state is eligible for additional incentive funds of $1,000 multiplied by the increased number of adoptions achieved by the state that are attributed to its improved adoption rate.[13]

However, increases due to improved adoption rates may only be paid if sufficient program funding is available after all awards for increases in the number of adoptions have been made.

Eligibility for Adoption Incentive Awards

Any state (includes the 50 states, District of Columbia, and Puerto Rico) operating a Title IV-E program may be eligible to earn Adoption Incentive funds provided awards are authorized for that year.[14] Current law authorizes awards for adoptions finalized in FY2008-FY2012—and authorizes funds for that purpose through FY2013.

Further, to be eligible for Adoption Incentives, the state must provide—via the Adoption and Foster Care Analysis Reporting System (AFCARS)—the necessary data to calculate the incentive amounts. The state must also assure that it provides health insurance coverage to any adoptive child for whom the state determined the child has special needs—including those eligible for ongoing Title IV-E adoption assistance and those with special needs who are not eligible for this assistance.[15] In addition, no state may receive an award for an increase in the number of special needs adoptions of children under the age of 9, unless that state has also shown an increase in that same year of the number of foster child or older child adoptions (compared to what the state achieved in FY2007), or an increase in the state's rate of adoption (compared to the rate achieved by the state in FY2002, or any subsequent year with a higher rate that is prior to the year the award is earned).

Awards and Appropriations

The first Adoption Incentive awards were paid in FY1999 for adoptions finalized in FY1998 and the most recent were paid in FY2012 for adoptions finalized in FY2011. During the life of the program, all 50 states, the District of Columbia and Puerto Rico have earned Adoption Incentive payments in one or more years and more than $375 million has been awarded to all states through FY2012. Discretionary funding is authorized for the program through FY2013 at the annual level of $43 million. Actual appropriation levels have varied and in recent years have been at roughly $39 million annually. Final FY2013 appropriations for the Adoption Incentives program were included in the Consolidated and Further Continuing Appropriations Act, 2013 (P.L. 113-6) at this same level. However, that appropriation is subject to a 5% reduction (under the March 1 sequestration order). Appropriations made as part of a given fiscal year's appropriation cycle are used to provide bonuses for increases in adoptions finalized in the previous fiscal year. For example, Adoption Incentives funding provided as part of the FY2012 appropriations cycle was awarded to states in August 2012 for adoptions finalized in FY2011. If not all of the funds available in the Adoption Incentive account are needed to make incentive awards, these funds may typically be carried over and used for bonus awards in a subsequent year.[16] Alternatively, if funding is not sufficient to make full bonus awards for increases in the *number of adoptions*, HHS pro-rates awards earned and, assuming appropriations are made for the subsequent year, will use some of the funds from that following year to pay the remainder of the incentives earned. However, bonus increases related to an improvement in the state's *rate of adoption* are only paid after all incentive awards for increase in the number of adoptions have been made and, then, only to the extent that funding is available when those awards are initially made. If insufficient funds are available at the time the initial incentive amounts are awarded, only part, or none, of these increases are paid.[17]

Table 1. Adoption Incentives: Summary of Appropriations and Award History

Appropriation Law	Appropriations	FY Adoptions Finalized	Award Amount
P.L. 105-277 (1999)	$19,994,999	FY1998 (35 states)	$42,510,000
P.L. 106-113 (2000)	$41,784,342	FY1999 (43 states and D.C.)	$51,488,000
P.L. 106-554 (2001)	$42,994,000	FY2000 (35 states and D.C.)	$33,238,000
P.L. 107-116 (2002)	$43,000,000	FY2001 (23 states and P.R.)	$17,578,000
P.L. 108-7 (2003)	$42,721,000[a]	FY2002 (25 states and P.R.)	$14,926,845
P.L. 108-199 (2004)	$7,456,000	FY2003 (31 states and P.R.)	$17,896,000
P.L. 108-447 (2005)	$9,346,000[b]	FY2004 (24 states, D.C. and P.R.)	$14,488,000
P.L. 109-149 (2006)	$17,808,000[a]	FY2005 (21 states)	$11,568,000
P.L. 110-7 (2007)	$5,000,000	FY2006 (19 states)	$7,354,000
P.L. 110-161 (2008)	$4,323,000	FY2007 (21 states)	$11,086,000
P.L. 111-8 (2009)	$36,500,000	FY2008 (38 states and D.C.)	$35,357,280[d]
P.L. 111-117(2010)	$39,500,000	FY2009 (38 states and P.R.)	$45,896,000[d]
P.L. 112-10 (2011)	$39,421,000	FY2010 (32 states)	$40,144,000[a]
P.L. 112-74 (2012)	$39,346,000	FY2011 (30 states)	$36,472,000[c,d]
P.L. 113-6 (2013)	$39,346,000[e]	*Awards for FY2012 adoptions expected to be made in late FY2013.*	
TOTAL appropriated *(includes some funds transferred, sequestration and therefore unavailable table notes)*	$414,012,341 *lapsed, or subject to for award; see*	TOTAL expected to be awarded *(includes amounts earned for FY2011increases adoptions for which funds were insufficient at award but which are expected to be paid)*[c,d]	$379,858,125 *in numbers of the time of the initial*[d]

Source: Table prepared by the Congressional Research Service (CRS) based on appropriations laws, HHS, ACF budget justifications, and CRS communication with ACF budget and program analysts who work on Adoption Incentives.

[a] Some of the funds provided in this appropriation cycle lapsed and were returned to the federal treasury. Funds may lapse when the Congressional authority for their use expires before they are needed to make incentive awards to states.

[b] The appropriation in P.L. 108-447 was initially $31.8 million. However, as part of FY2006 appropriations (P.L. 109-149), Congress rescinded $22.5 million of that funding. In addition, HHS/ACF exercised its discretion to move 1% of the appropriated funds ($318,000) to the Refugee and Entrant Assistance program. This additionally reduced the total FY2005 funds available for Adoption Incentives to $9.0 million, although the amount shown in the table reflects funding after the rescission and prior to the transfer.

[c] This is the total amount of funds states earned for increases in the numbers of adoptions finalized in FY2011. When it issued initial bonus funds for FY2011 adoptions (in August 2012), HHS had Adoption Incentive funding available to award 87% of this

amount ($31.8 million). However, if HHS follows its past practice, states can expect to receive the remaining $4.7 million out of FY2013 program appropriations.

[d] The award amounts shown in the final column of this table include increases tied to improved adoption rates only if those increases were paid to states. Beginning with adoptions finalized in FY2008-FY2011, states were eligible for increases in their Adoption Incentive awards if they improved their rate of adoptions. However, Section 473A(d)(3) of the Social Security Act provides that these awards may only be paid if funds remain available after any awards for increases in the *number* of adoptions are made. Funding was available to provide 48% ($1.7 million) of total increases ($3.5 million) calculated for improved FY2008 adoption rates. No funds were available to provide awards for any part of the increases for which states with improved adoption rates were eligible in FY2009 ($3.5 million), FY2010 ($2.3 million) or FY2011 ($0.9 million).

[e] This appropriation is subject to the March 1 sequestration order, which is expected to reduce funding by 5%.

Table 1 summarizes the appropriations provided and awards made by fiscal year for which the funds were initially appropriated and the fiscal year for which the incentive funds were earned. For numerous years, not all of the funding shown as the award amount for a given year was actually paid to states at a single time or in a single fiscal year. However, with the exception of FY2011 (discussed below), the total award amount shown was eventually paid once additional funding was provided for the program. For adoptions finalized in FY2011, 87% ($31.8 million) of the total award amount shown in Table 1 ($36.5 million) was available to be awarded in FY2012. However, the additional $4.7 million is expected to be awarded to states in FY2013 (using FY2013 appropriations and before awards for adoptions finalized in FY2012 are made).

Awards by Category for Adoptions Finalized in FY2008-FY2011

Under the incentive structure used to make awards for adoptions finalized in FY2008-FY2011, states were eligible to receive $166 million and were expected to receive a total of $158 million in Adoption Incentive payments.

As of the end of FY2012, states had been paid 97% ($151 million) of the $156 million they earned for increasing the *numbers* of adoptions finalized in FY2008-FY2011. They are expected to receive the remaining 3% of the bonus amounts tied to increased number of adoptions, out of the FY2013 appropriation made for the Adoption Incentives program. By contrast, while states are *eligible* for increases in their adoption incentive payments when they improve on their highest-ever adoption rate, those additional incentive amounts may only be paid when the program funding exceeds what is needed to pay awards tied to increases in the number of adoptions. Therefore, although states were eligible for additional bonus payments of $10.2 million— for improving their adoption rates in award years FY2008-FY2011—they were paid only a fraction of that total (16% or $1.7 million) and no more of that total is to be paid.[18] Under the current incentive structure, 44 states were paid Adoption Incentives bonus payments in one or more award category for adoptions finalized in any of FY2008-FY2011.[19] Among the eight states that were not paid an incentive for adoptions finalized in those years, five (Colorado, Massachusetts, New Jersey, Ohio, and Vermont) actually increased their *rate* of adoption in one or more of those award years and therefore were eligible for an adoption incentive payment, but did not receive an award due to the program funding level. Additionally, one state (New York) increased the number of special needs (under age 9) adoptions in three of those four years. However, because it did not earn an incentive in any of the other categories (foster child, older child, or adoption rate), it was not eligible for incentive funds for those increases. The remaining two states (District of Columbia and Iowa) did not increase the number of adoptions achieved or improve their rates of adoption in any of the four years.

Table 2 shows the total amounts paid (or expected to be paid) to states under the current incentive structure by award year and incentive category. States did not necessarily receive all of these bonus payments in a single fiscal year. Further, there were insufficient program funds available to pay bonuses for improved adoption rates in most years. Therefore the total amount of bonus payments that states were eligible to receive for adoptions finalized in FY2008-FY2011 is about $8 million more than the total amount they were expected to receive. (For incentive awards by category and for each state, see Table D-5 in Appendix D.)

Foster Child Adoptions

States earned bonus payments of $74.5 million (45% of the total bonuses they were eligible to receive) for increasing their number of foster child adoptions finalized in FY2008-FY2011. That award category is the broadest— applying to children adopted from foster care generally. States may earn $4,000 for every adoption of a foster child in the given award year that is above the number of foster child adoptions the state completed in FY2007 (the baseline year). Sixteen states finalized more foster child adoptions in each of FY2008-FY2011 than they did in FY2007, and they earned foster child adoption bonuses in each of these four years. Half of the states (26) earned incentives for increases in foster child adoptions in at least one of the four years, and 10 states did not improve on their FY2007 record in any of these four years. (For information by state see Table D-1 in Appendix D.)

Table 2. Adoption Incentives for Adoptions
Completed in FY2008–FY2011
Dollars in millions; summed parts may not equal totals due to rounding

Incentive Category	FY2008	FY2009	FY2010	FY2011	Total
Foster Child	$16.1	$23.4	$18.9	$16.0	*$74.5*
Older Child (9 years or older)	$8.7	$12.0	$12.5	$11.8	*$44.9*
Special Needs (under 9 years)	$8.9	$10.3	$8.8	$8.7	*$36.7*
Adoption Rate	$3.5	$3.5	$2.3	$.09	*$10.2*
*TOTAL incentives for which states were eligible*a	*$37.1*	*$49.3*	*$42.4*	*$37.4*	*$166.3*
TOTAL incentives paid or expected to be paidb	$35.4	$45.8	$40.1	$36.5	$157.7

Source: Table prepared by the Congressional Research Service (CRS) based on data provided by HHS, Children's Bureau.

[a] Beginning with FY2008, states are eligible for additional incentive sums based on improvements to their adoption rate *if sufficient appropriations are available to pay these awards after awards are made for increases in the numbers of adoptions.* FY2008 was the only year for which some funds were available for increases due to states' improved adoption rates. Eligible states were paid $1.7 million or about 48% of the $3.5 million in incentive amounts tied to improved adoption rates achieved that year. There were no funds available for incentives tied to adoption rate improvements in FY2009 ($3.5 million), FY2010 ($2.3 million), and FY2011 ($898,000).

[b] Adoption Incentive awards are typically made at the end of the fiscal year for adoptions finalized in the previous fiscal year and after any unpaid awards tied to increases in the *number of* adoptions finalized in an earlier year. For example, HHS used FY2012 adoption incentive appropriations to complete bonus payments to states for increases in the number of adoptions finalized in FY2010. After those payments were made there was just $31.8 million remaining available from the FY2012 appropriations to make awards for adoptions finalized in FY2011. States received that amount (on a pro-rated basis) in August 2012. However, assuming HHS follows past practice, states are expected to be paid an additional $4.7 million (i.e., the remaining bonus amounts tied to increases in the *number* of adoptions finalized in FY2011) out of the FY2013 Adoption Incentives appropriations (and before any awards for adoptions finalized in FY2012 are made with those funds).

Older Child Adoptions

Twenty-seven percent ($44.9 million) of the total bonus dollars states were eligible to receive for adoptions finalized in FY2008-FY2011 were tied to increases in the number of children who were adopted at 9 years of age or older. Adoptions of older children are less common than are adoptions of those who are younger. However, states may earn the largest award amount for increases in this incentive category. Specifically, states may earn $8,000 for every adoption of an "older child" in the given award year that is above the number of older child adoptions the state completed in FY2007 (the baseline year). Fifteen states earned incentives for increasing their numbers of older child adoptions in each of FY2008-FY2011 and close to half of the states (25) did so in at least one of those four years. Twelve states did not increase their number of older child adoptions (above their FY2007 level in the state) in any of those four years. (For information by state see Table D-2 in Appendix D.)

Special Needs (under Age 9) Adoptions

Twenty-two percent ($36.7 million) of the bonus funds states were eligible to receive for adoptions finalized in FY2008-FY2011 were linked to increases in the number of adoptions of children who were determined to have special needs and who were under the age of nine. States are only eligible to earn bonus funds in this category if they have earned an award in at least one other incentive category during the same fiscal year (i.e., they increased older child or foster child adoptions or they improved their rate of adoption). For eligible states, the award amount is $4,000 for every adoption of a special needs child under 9 years of age that is above the state's baseline number of such adoptions (i.e., above the number of such adoptions it achieved in FY2007).

For adoptions finalized in FY2008-FY2011, ten states increased their number of special needs (under age 9) adoptions above their baseline, but were not eligible in one or more years when this occurred because they did not earn a bonus in any other Adoption Incentive category in that same year. Overall, ten states earned bonus funds for increases in the number of special needs (under age 9) adoptions finalized in each of FY2008-FY2011; close to half of the states (24) did so in at least one of the four years; and 18 states did not earn an award in this category in any of those four years (either because they didn't increase the number of these adoptions or because they did not earn an incentive in any other award category). (For information by state see Table D-3 in Appendix D.)

Adoption Rate

Finally, the total bonus amount a state is eligible to receive in a year is increased if the state improves its rate of adoption. However, this increased bonus amount is only authorized to be paid to states if sufficient appropriations remain available *after* awards are made for increases in the number of adoptions. For adoptions finalized in FY2008-FY2011, states were eligible for $10.2 million in bonus payments for improved adoption rates (6% of bonus payments states were eligible for across all four award categories). However, there were sufficient appropriations to award just $1.7 million of this amount.

A state's adoption rate is equal to the total number of foster child adoptions it completed in the fiscal year for every 100 children that were in its foster care caseload on the last day of the preceding fiscal year. An award for an increased rate of adoption can ensure that an incentive may be earned by a state that continues to appropriately move children from foster care to adoption even as the total number of children in foster care declines. In those states, the total number of children for whom adoption is the desired or appropriate permanency outcome is also likely to decline.

To be counted as having an improved adoption rate, a state was required to exceed the highest rate of adoptions it had achieved in any year (beginning with FY2002) that came before the year for which the awards were being calculated. A state that improved its adoption rate was eligible for $1,000 award for each adoption calculated to have been achieved due to the higher rate of adoptions.

The large majority of states (43) improved on their initial adoption rate baseline in one or more years from FY2008-FY2011. In FY2008, on average, states finalized roughly 11 adoptions for every 100 children who were in foster care; the comparable number for FY2011 was approaching 13 adoptions for every 100 children in foster care. (For information by state see Table D-4 in Appendix D.)

Spending Award Money

States may spend Adoption Incentive funds anytime within a 24-month period, beginning with the month in which the funds are awarded to a state.[20] The statute permits states to spend these bonus dollars on any service authorized to be provided to children and families under Title IV-B or Title IV-E of the Social Security Act. Those parts of the law authorize a broad range of child welfare-related activities, including activities to prevent child abuse or neglect and/or provide services to enable a child to remain in his/her own home; investigation of alleged child abuse or neglect and placement of children in foster care if necessary; provision of services to reunite a child in foster care with his/her parents and for services to maintain the reunification; finding a new permanent home for children who may not be reunited with their parents, including through adoption or guardianship; provision of post-permanency services; and services to assist a youth in foster care to make a successful transition to adulthood. A state may not count its spending of Adoption Incentive funds toward meeting any of the "matching" requirements included in the programs authorized in Title IV-E and Title IV-B of the Social Security Act. (Programs under those parts of the law generally require states to supply between 20% -50% of the total program funding out of its non-federal, state or local, dollars.)[21]

Many states report spending incentive funds on adoption-related purposes, including post-adoption support services (e.g., support for adoptive parent mentors or adoptive family support groups, respite care, casework and supports for adoptive families of children at risk of re-entering foster care); recruitment of adoptive homes (e.g., support for online adoption exchange or photo-listing, development of promotional materials, child-specific recruitment efforts); and training or conferences to improve adoption casework.

Other adoption-related services or supports funded with Adoption Incentive awards (in a smaller number of states) included provision of monthly adoption assistance payments, purchase of new equipment or provision of other resources to improve processing and archiving of adoption records, support for new or improved adoption home studies, and attention to inter-jurisdictional adoption placement. Some states used Adoption Incentive funds for foster care-related activities (e.g., training or recruitment of foster parents— alone or in combination with adoptive parents and foster and/or adoptive parent supports). Others referenced support for permanency efforts more generally (i.e., incorporating guardianship or reunification). At least one state reported using these incentive funds for foster care maintenance payments.

Finally, a few states described use of Adoption Incentive funds for services to families and children remaining in the home (e.g., alternative response and direct child protection services).[22]

SELECTED REAUTHORIZATION ISSUES

From its inception in 1997, the Adoption Incentives program has sought to encourage permanency for more children by rewarding states that increase the number of adoptions of children who would otherwise have no permanent family to call their own. In considering its reauthorization Congress may want to examine the continued need for and purpose of incentives for adoption, as well as, the particular focus and structure of any continued program. Selected issues are discussed below.

Continued Need for and Focus of Incentives

Since the 1997 enactment of ASFA, including the Adoption Incentives program, the number and rate of adoptions from foster care has increased significantly and the length of time needed to complete those adoptions has decreased. Given these successes, Congress might consider whether there is a continued need for this incentive program. On the other hand—given that each year many more children remain in foster care waiting for adoptions than are adopted, and also that many thousands of youth age out of state custody (26,000 in FY2011) without being safely reunited with biological parents or placed in a new permanent family—Congress may seek to continue the program with adjustments. For example, Congress could provide incentives to states for successful exits from foster care to permanent families of any kind (e.g., safe return to biological family and/or legal guardianship with a family, in addition to adoption). Alternatively, Congress could continue to exclusively support exits to adoption but it could refocus the kinds of categories for which states receive awards. For example, Congress could limit awards to successful adoption of the hardest to place children exclusively, such as older youth (particularly those entering care at an older age), children or youth with multiple foster care placements, or those with mental health challenges.

Permanence for Older Children

Youth who leave foster care without placement in a permanent family are at high-risk for homelessness, poor job outcomes, low educational attainment, and other negative outcomes.[23] Beginning with adoptions finalized in FY2004, the Adoption Incentives program offered states particular incentives for the adoption of children who are age 9 or older. These children are referred to as "older" in the Adoption Incentives program. Despite this incentive, older child adoptions remain less common than those of younger children. Among children adopted from foster care, 31% were age nine or older in FY2004 and in FY2011 that share was just 26%. In addition, many older children continue to leave foster care without placement in a permanent family. Among youth who left foster care in FY2004 and were age 15 or older, 21,600 were emancipated and an additional 4,200 were formally discharged with an exit reason of "runaway." The comparable figures in FY2011 were 24,300 and 1,300.

Congress may consider ways to further adjust the incentive structure or make other changes designed to reduce the number of youth who leave care without placement in a permanent family. As discussed by witnesses at a February 27, 2013 hearing held by the Subcommittee on Human Resources of the House Ways and Means Committee, ensuring adoption (or permanence via guardianship) is possible but may require specific kinds of recruitment efforts, youth engagement in the process, belief on the part of caseworkers that permanence can be achieved for these youth and more limited or different use of the case plan goal "another planned permanent living arrangement (APPLA)" for older youth. (For more discussion see "Related Legislative Actions in the 113th Congress.")

Baseline Adjustment

Congress may consider whether to adjust the baselines used to determine whether a state has achieved an increase in the number of foster child, older child, or special needs under age 9 adoptions. Throughout the program history, the incentive structure has been adjusted by Congress to update the award structure to ensure continued incentive for states to increase adoptions from foster care. (See Appendix C.)

Currently states must achieve a higher number of adoptions than they achieved in FY2007 to be eligible for awards in the foster child, older child, or special needs under age 9 award categories. Nationally, between FY2007 and FY2011, the number of children in foster care declined by 18% (from 510,000 to 401,000) and the number of those children in foster care who were counted as "waiting for adoption" declined by 22% (from 134,000 to 104,000).[24] While the amount and kind of change in the foster child and "waiting" population varied greatly by state, only six states saw an increase in their foster care caseload from the last day of FY2007 to the last day of FY2011 and just eight saw an increase in the number of children waiting for adoption. (See Table E-1 and Table E-2 in Appendix E.)

A declining number of children for whom adoption is appropriate makes it more difficult to exceed an absolute number of adoptions that were achieved in a state when that number of children was larger. The 2008 reauthorization of the Adoption Incentives program sought to address this concern, in part, by moving the "baseline" year closer to the year for which the award is to be determined. Separately, it authorized some awards based on improved adoption rates as discussed below.

Availability of Awards for Improved Rate of Adoption

Calculating a state's rate of adoption—that is the number of foster child adoptions in a given year for every 100 children in foster care on the last day of the prior fiscal year—effectively holds constant the size of the state's foster care caseload and thus provides a view of a state's success at completing adoptions that is independent of any change in the size of its foster care caseload. Congress introduced this new award category as part of the FY2008 reauthorization of the Adoption Incentive Program. However, although nearly every state improved its rate of adoption since this award category was established (see Table D-4 in Appendix D) only 1% of all bonus funds expected to be paid for adoptions in FY2008 through FY2011 were tied to adoption rate increases. The reasons for this include the following:

- The size of the award for a rate increase ($1,000), which is just one-quarter of the award amount offered for increases in the number of foster child or special needs under age 9 adoptions and one-eighth of the amount offered for older child adoptions.
- The stipulation that awards for adoption rate increases may only be paid once states receive all award amounts earned for an absolute increase in the *number* of children adopted. (There have been sufficient funds to pay just $1.7 million of the total $10.2 million in increased bonuses states were eligible for due to rate increases since this award category was established.)
- The fact that the baseline for this award category changes to a higher rate each year the state makes an improvement in its adoption rate. (By contrast, the baselines for increases in each of the number of

adoption award categories are fixed at the state's level of success in FY2007.)

Use of Incentive Funds

States may spend Adoption Incentive funds they receive for any of the range of child welfare services authorized under Title IV-B or Title IV-E of the Social Security Act and they may not count these funds as "non-federal" dollars for purposes of providing required matching dollars under any of those programs. The Administration, as part of its FY2014 budget request for reauthorization of the Adoption Incentive program, proposes requiring states to spend any of these bonus funds on "trauma-informed services to improve social and emotional well-being of children waiting for adoption or those having achieved adoption."[25] Congress might consider narrowing the purposes on which states might spend incentive funds. For example, they might limit use of the awards to post-permanency-related supports or to the trauma-informed services proposed by the Administration. Additionally, or alone, they might stipulate certain activities that may not be supported with these funds (e.g., foster care maintenance, adoption assistance, or guardianship assistance payments). On the other hand, given that bonus funds are by their nature less predictable than other kinds of federal grants, and the fact that states have earned the bonus by improved performance, Congress might choose to retain the current flexibility states have in the use of these funds.

RELATED LEGISLATIVE ACTIONS IN THE 113TH CONGRESS

On February 27, 2013, the Subcommittee on Human Resources of the House Ways and Means Committee held a hearing on "Increasing Adoptions from Foster Care." Subcommittee Chairman Dave Reichert, noting the increase in adoptions and decline in the foster care caseload since the enactment of the Adoption Incentives program and other changes to the law in 1997, said that the hearing was to consider if other changes were needed to encourage adoption from foster care.[26] Four witnesses discussed the importance of adoption as a way for children to find permanent homes and they gave particular attention to the need for adoptions of older children and those with special needs. Each of the witnesses supported reauthorization of the Adoption Incentives program.

Several witnesses described successful efforts to recruit adoptive families for older or harder to place children as those that start with a focus on the individual children or youth in need of families and engage them in the search for those families. [27] One recruitment model, known as "Wendy's Wonderful Kids" includes small caseloads that allow adoption caseworkers to get to know and work with the children for whom they are seeking permanent homes. A rigorous study of the model's effectiveness found that children served under this recruitment and placement model were one and a half times more likely to leave foster care for permanent homes then those who received traditional adoptive home recruitment services. The model's impact is greatest among older children and those with mental health disorders.[28] The state of Ohio has recently contracted to use the Wendy's Wonderful Kids model (on a nearly statewide basis) to find homes for harder to place children age 9 or older. By moving children from foster care to permanent homes more quickly, Ohio anticipates significant fiscal savings. [29]

Raising awareness of the need for adoptive families is a central goal of the Wait No More campaign, discussed by another hearing witness. This campaign brings together public child welfare agencies, private and public adoption agencies, church leaders and other support partners to promote and host adoption events at churches around the country. Interested families may begin the adoption process at the event, where speakers stress that adoption is about meeting the needs of the child (not the needs of adults), discuss common behavioral challenges for adoptees from foster care, and, offer strategies to enable successful child and family outcomes. [30]

Witnesses also focused on the need for post-adoption services, including counselors with specific training and knowledge about the needs of adoptive families, to ensure safety and stability of these families.[31] One witness asked that the longer-standing federal focus and financial support for increasing adoptions be coupled with a greater focus on (and financial support for) post-adoption services and suggested that Congress require states to spend their Adoption Incentive funds on post-adoption support.[32] Another asked that Congress ensure that children who were adopted did not lose access to education, mental health-related or other services that would be available to them if they remained in foster care.[33]

Several witnesses mentioned assignment of the case plan goal "another planned permanent living arrangement" (APPLA) as a potential barrier to finding permanent families for youth in care.[34] Once a youth's goal is fixed as "APPLA," one witness noted the child welfare agency stops searching for a permanent family and focuses exclusively on preparing the youth for "independent living." He asserted that federal policy should always require efforts to find a permanent home for youth in care and noted that those efforts could continue even as the agency worked to help the youth develop independent living skills.[35]

Other issues raised at the hearing included a call for reauthorization of the separate competitive grant program known as Family Connections,[36], [37] which one witness noted supports projects that can help connect youth with permanent families through greater kinship support, intensive family-finding efforts and family group decision-making meetings, and greater use (by states) of Title IV-E training funds to support more competent adoption casework.[38] As part of the hearing question and answer, witnesses also supported expanding the Adoption Incentives program to reward states that help youth gain a safe, permanent family through means other than adoption. In particular, several mentioned the importance of legal guardianship to achieving a permanent family for some older youth.[39]

APPENDIX A. GLOSSARY OF TERMS

ADOPTION RATE—The number of children in foster care who are adopted during a fiscal year for every 100 children who were in foster care on the last day of the previous fiscal year.

ADOPTION RATE BASELINE—Highest ever adoption rate achieved by the state for any fiscal year that is before the fiscal year for which the Adoption Incentive rate award is being determined, beginning with FY2002.

ANOTHER PLANNED PERMANENT LIVING ARRANGEMENT (APPLA)—Each child in foster care must have a permanency goal—that is a plan for leaving foster care to a permanent home. A hearing to determine (or re-determine) that permanency goal must be held no later than 12 months after a child enters foster care, and every 12 months thereafter while the child remains in foster care. If at this hearing it is determined that the child's plan for permanency may not be any of reuniting with his/her parents, placement for adoption, placement with a legal guardian, or going to live with a fit and willing relative, then a child's plan for exiting care may be "another planned permanent living arrangement."

BASELINE (as used in the Adoption Incentive program)—The standard against which state performance is measured to determine whether, in a given year, the state has increased its number of adoptions or improved its adoption rate. A baseline is specific to the state, and is based on a state's past performance. (The four specific baselines used in the current Adoption Incentives program are defined individually in this glossary.)

FOSTER CHILD ADOPTION—The finalized adoption of a child who, at the time of adoptive placement, was in public foster care under the placement and care responsibility of the state child welfare agency.

FOSTER CHILD ADOPTION BASELINE—The number of foster child adoptions in the state in FY2007 as reported by the state via the Adoption and Foster Care Analysis Reporting System (AFCARS).

GUARDIANSHIP—A judicially created legal relationship between child and caretaker which is intended to be permanent and self-sustaining as evidenced by the transfer to the caretaker of the following parental rights with respect to the child: protection, education, care and control of the person, custody of the person, and decision-making.

OLDER CHILD ADOPTION—The finalized adoption of a child who is nine years of age or older and who, at the time of the adoptive placement was in public foster care *or* was the subject of a Title IV-E adoption assistance agreement between the state child welfare agency and the child's adoptive parents.

OLDER CHILD ADOPTION BASELINE - The number of older child adoptions in the state in FY2007 as reported by the state via AFCARS.

SPECIAL NEEDS ADOPTION– The adoption of a child whom the state has determined (1) cannot be returned to his or her parents and (2) is unlikely to be adopted without assistance because of a particular factor or condition (e.g., child's age; membership in a sibling group; minority race/ethnicity; medical or physical condition; or emotional, mental or behavioral disability). Additionally, unless this is not in the best interest of the child, the state must have made reasonable efforts to place the child for adoption without providing assistance. (A state is required to enter into a Title IV-E adoption assistance agreement with the adoptive parents of any child it finds to have special needs.)

SPECIAL NEEDS (UNDER AGE 9) ADOPTION—The finalized adoption of a child who is eight years of age or younger and who at the time of the adoptive placement was the subject of a Title IV-E adoption assistance agreement between the state child welfare agency and the child's adoptive parents.

SPECIAL NEEDS (UNDER AGE 9) ADOPTION BASELINE—The number of special needs (under age 9) adoptions in the state in FY2007 as reported by the state via AFCARS.

TERMINATION OF PARENTAL RIGHTS (TPR)—The legal severing (in a state court /court of competent jurisdiction) of the parent-child relationship. (Typically this severs the rights and responsibilities of a biological parent to his/her child. In the case of a previously adopted child however, it is the severing of the rights and responsibilities of the adoptive parent.)

WAITING FOR ADOPTION (as counted by HHS, Children's Bureau)—A child who is in foster care and who has a case plan goal of adoption and/or to whom all parental rights have been terminated. Except that any youth age 16 or older and to whom all parental rights have been terminated is excluded *if* that youth has a case plan goal of "emancipation."

APPENDIX B. TRENDS IN ADOPTIONS WITH PUBLIC CHILD WELFARE AGENCY INVOLVEMENT

Table B-1 shows, by fiscal year, the number of adoptions in which the public child welfare agency was involved, the number of children in foster care (under the responsibility of the public child welfare agency) on the last day of the fiscal year, and the rate of adoptions. All children who leave public foster care for adoption are adopted with public child welfare agency involvement and they represent the very large number of children shown in the adoption column. A small number of children who do not enter foster care may also be adopted with public child welfare agency involvement and that number is also included in the number shown in the adoptions column.

Table B-1. Adoptions with Public Child Welfare Agency Involvement, FY1995-FY2011

Fiscal Year	Children in Public Foster Care *on the last day of the fiscal year*	Public Agency-Involved Adoptions *during the fiscal year*	Adoption Rate
1995	483,000	25,700	5.5
1996	507,000	27,800	5.7
1997	537,000	31,000	6.1
1998	559,000	38,000	7.1
1999	567,000	46,900	8.4
2000	552,000	51,100	9.0
2001	545,000	50,600	9.2

Table B-1. (Continued)

Fiscal Year	Children in Public Foster Care *on the last day of the fiscal year*	Public Agency-Involved Adoptions *during the fiscal year*	Adoption Rate
2002	523,000	51,400	9.4
2003	510,000	49,600	9.5
2004	508,000	51,000	10.0
2005	511,000	51,600	10.2
2006	505,000	50,600	9.9
2007	482,000	52,700	10.4
2008	464,000	55,200	11.5
2009	422,000	57,100	12.3
2010	406,000	53,600	12.7
2011	401,000	50,500	12.4

Source: Table prepared by the Congressional Research Service. Children in foster care based on Table 11-4, "Additional Tables and Figures," Chapter 11, U.S. House Ways and Means Committee, *2012, Green Book*. Adoptions (based on Table 11-56 in *2008 Green Book* (for FY2001 and earlier years) and HHS, Children's Bureau, "Adoptions of Children with Public Child Welfare Agency Involvement by State" posted in June 2011(for FY2002) and July 2012 (for FY2003-FY2012).

Note: Data are displayed rounded to nearest 1,000 for total caseload and nearest 100 for adoptions. However, whenever more exact numbers were available they were used to compute the rate shown.

Adoption Rate = Number of public child welfare agency adoptions in the given fiscal year for every 100 children in foster care on the last day of the preceding fiscal year.

Table B-2. Number of Children Waiting for Adoption and Percentage of Waiting Children Adopted, FY1998-FY2011

Fiscal Year	Children Waiting for Adoption *on last day of the fiscal year*	Percentage of Waiting Children Adopted *Children adopted in given fiscal year as percentage of waiting children on last day of previous fiscal year*
1998	125,000	*not available*[a]
1999	130,000	37%
2000	131,000	39%
2001	130,100	39%
2002	133,900	40%
2003	130,600	37%
2004	130,400	39%

Fiscal Year	Children Waiting for Adoption on last day of the fiscal year	Percentage of Waiting Children Adopted Children adopted in given fiscal year as percentage of waiting children on last day of previous fiscal year
2005	130,700	40%
2006	135,400	39%
2007	133,700	39%
2008	125,700	41%
2009	114,500	45%
2010	109,500	47%
2011	104,200	46%

Source: Table prepared by the Congressional Research Services based on data reported by states via AFCARS and provided to CRS by HHS, Children's Bureau.

Notes: Number of children waiting for adoption is displayed rounded to nearest 100. However, whenever a more exact number was available, it was used to calculate the percentage. There is no definition of "waiting children" in statute or regulation. For purposes of analysis, the HHS, Children's Bureau counts as "waiting" each child in foster care on the last day of the fiscal year who has a case plan goal of adoption and/or for whom all parental rights have been terminated. However, it *excludes* from this number any youth in care who is age 16 or older for whom all parental rights have been terminated if that youth's case plan goal is "emancipation."

[a] Could not be calculated because there is no estimate of the number of waiting children in FY1997.

Table B-3. Average and Median Length of Time to Finalized Adoption, In Months, FY2000-FY2011

Fiscal Year	Months from Removal to Termination of Parental Rights (TPR) *(Among children later adopted)*		Months from Termination of Parental Rights (TPR) to Adoption		TOTAL TIME TO FINALIZE ADOPTION *Months from removal to adoption*	
	Average	*Median*	*Average*	*Median*	*Average*	*Median*
2000	32.3	26.0	15.9	12.0	45.9	39.3
2001	29.7	23.5	16.0	11.8	44.0	37.5
2002	27.8	21.5	16.1	12.0	42.9	35.9
2003	26.1	20.1	16.2	12.0	41.8	34.9
2004	24.4	19.3	15.8	11.3	40.3	33.5
2005	23.4	18.8	15.0	10.7	38.3	32.0
2006	22.3	18.4	14.6	10.5	36.9	31.1
2007	21.6	17.9	14.1	10.3	35.7	30.3

Table B-3. (Continued)

Fiscal Year	Months from Removal to Termination of Parental Rights (TPR) *(Among children later adopted)*		Months from Termination of Parental Rights (TPR) to Adoption		TOTAL TIME TO FINALIZE ADOPTION *Months from removal to adoption*	
	Average	*Median*	*Average*	*Median*	*Average*	*Median*
2008	21.0	17.7	14.3	10.5	35.2	30.2
2009	20.8	17.8	14.1	10.3	34.8	30.3
2010	20.6	17.7	13.8	10.0	34.6	30.0
2011	20.1	17.4	13.7	9.8	34.0	29.2

Source: Table prepared by the Congressional Research Service based on state-reported
   AFCARS data (as of August 2012) provided to CRS by HHS, Children's Bureau.
Note:
The median length of time to adoption measures the point at which half of the children
   adopted in the given fiscal year reached a finalized adoption in fewer months and
   half in more.
By contrast, an average combines the total months to adoptions for all children with a
   finalized adoption in the given fiscal year and divides that number by the total
   number of adoptions.
The average time to adoption is considerably longer than the median time to adoption
   because the average is affected by children with significantly longer stays in foster
   care.

APPENDIX C.
ADOPTION INCENTIVE
BONUS STRUCTURE

At each reauthorization of the Adoption Incentives program, Congress has
adjusted the bonus structure.

New award categories and adjustments to the baselines have placed
greater emphasis on adoption of harder to place children, helped to ensure that
earning an incentive was possible even as caseloads declined, and protected
the value of the incentives from erosion by inflation.

Table C-1. Evolution of Adoption Incentives Bonus Structure

NA = not authorized

Bonus Structure	Original Structure *Adoption and Safe Families Act of 1997, P.L. 105-89*	Initial Amendment *Adoption Promotion Act of 2003, P.L. 108-145*	Current Structure *Fostering Connections and Increasing Adoptions Act of 2008, P.L. 110-351*
Award category	*Foster Child:* Increase in number of children adopted from foster care.	*Foster Child:* Same as prior law.	*Foster Child:* Same as prior law.
	Special Needs: Increase in number of children adopted who are determined to have "special needs."	*Special Needs Under Age 9:* Increase in number of children adopted who are determined to have special needs [b] and are younger than 9 years of age.	*Special Needs Under Age 9:* Same as prior law.
	NA	*Older Child:* Increase in number of older children (age 9 years or above) adopted.	*Older Child:* Same as prior law.
	NA	NA	*Adoption Rate:* Increase in rate of children adopted from foster care (where rate equals the state's number of foster child adoptions in a fiscal year for every 100 children in foster care in that state on the last day of the previous fiscal year).

Table C-1. (Continued)

	Original Structure *Adoption and Safe Families Act of 1997, P.L. 105-89*	Initial Amendment *Adoption Promotion Act of 2003, P.L. 108-145*	Current Structure *Fostering Connections and Increasing Adoptions Act of 2008, P.L. 110-351*
Bonus Structure			
Baselines Number	*Adoptions finalized in FY1998:* For each award category, the average number of adoptions achieved by the state in that category for FY1995-FY1997. *Adoptions finalized in FY1999-FY2002:* For each award category, the highest number of adoptions finalized by the state in that category in FY1997 or the highest number in any following fiscal year that precedes the year for which the award is being determined.	*Adoptions finalized in FY2003- FY2007:* For each award category, the highest number of adoptions finalized by the state in that category in FY2002 or the highest number in any following fiscal year that precedes the year for which the award is being determined.	*Adoptions finalized in FY2008 - FY2012:* For each award category, the number of adoptions finalized by the state in that award category during FY2007.
Rate	NA	NA	*Adoptions finalized in FY2008 - FY2012:* The highest rate of foster child adoptions achieved by the state in FY2002 or the highest rate achieved in any following fiscal year that precedes the year for which the award is being determined.

	Original Structure Adoption and Safe Families Act of 1997, P.L. 105-89	Initial Amendment Adoption Promotion Act of 2003, P.L. 108-145	Current Structure Fostering Connections and Increasing Adoptions Act of 2008, P.L. 110-351
Bonus Structure			
Bonus Amounts	Foster Child: $4,000 for every foster child adoption above the state's baseline.	Foster Child: Same as prior law.	Foster Child: Same as prior law.
	Special Needs: $2,000 for every special needs adoption above the state's baseline. (Except that a state may only earn a bonus in this category if it also earned a bonus for increases in foster child adoptions.)	Special Needs under age 9: $2,000 for every special needs under age nine adoption above the state's baseline. (Except that a state may only earn a bonus in this category if it also earned a bonus for increases in either foster child or older child adoptions.)	Special Needs under age 9: $4,000 for every special needs under age nine adoption above the state's baseline. (Except that a state may only earn a bonus in this category if it also earned a bonus for increases in either foster child or older child adoptions or if it improved its adoption rate.)
	NA	Older Child: $4,000 for every older child adoption above the state's baseline.	Older Child: $8,000 for every older child adoption above the state's baseline.
	NA	NA	Adoption Rate: $1,000 for every adoption finalized that is attributed to the state's higher rate of adoption. (States may only receive bonus funds in this award category if sufficient funds remain available to make the award after all bonuses have been paid for any increases in foster child, older child, and special needs under age 9 adoptions.)

Source: Table prepared by the Congressional Research Service.

APPENDIX D. ADOPTIONS AND INCENTIVES EARNED BY CATEGORY AND STATE

Table D-1. Foster Child Adoptions and Incentives Earned for FY2008-FY2011

Initial incentive awards are paid in the fiscal year following the year in which the incentive was earned

State	Baseline Number of Foster child adoptions in FY2007	Number of Foster Child Adoptions Finalized in				Incentives Earned for Foster Child Adoptions Finalized in			
		FY2008	FY2009	FY2010	FY2011	FY2008	FY2009	FY2010	FY2011
Alabama	349	402	624	606	439	$212,000	$1,100,000	$1,028,000	$360,000
Alaska	244	261	338	336	292	$68,000	$376,000	$368,000	$192,000
Arizona	1,565	1,596	1,636	2,045	2,243	$124,000	$284,000	$1,920,000	$2,712,000
Arkansas	401	498	591	589	589	$388,000	$760,000	$752,000	$752,000
California	7,622	7,777	7,033	5,644	5,007	$620,000	$0	$0	$0
Colorado	1,077	995	1,057	968	930	$0	$0	$0	$0
Connecticut	569	647	684	564	505	$312,000	$460,000	$0	$0
Delaware	118	111	125	67	95	$0	$28,000	$0	$0
District of Columbia	151	111	99	127	104	$0	$0	$0	$0
Florida	2,970	3,959	3,763	3,243	2,899	$3,956,000	$3,172,000	$1,092,000	$0
Georgia	1,237	1,265	1,242	1,193	1,060	$112,000	$20,000	$0	$0
Hawaii	242	257	265	209	192	$60,000	$92,000	$0	$0
Idaho	190	229	338	306	254	$156,000	$592,000	$464,000	$256,000
Illinois	1,512	1,527	1,414	1,214	482[a]	$60,000	$0	$0	$0
Indiana	1,278	1,506	1,562	1,458	1,554	$912,000	$1,136,000	$720,000	$1,104,000
Iowa	1,060	1,038	1,005	795	851	$0	$0	$0	$0

State	Baseline *Number of Foster child adoptions in FY2007*	Number of Foster Child Adoptions Finalized in				Incentives Earned for Foster Child Adoptions Finalized in			
		FY2008	FY2009	FY2010	FY2011	FY2008	FY2009	FY2010	FY2011
Kansas	*777*	704	863	685	777	$0	$344,000	$0	$0
Kentucky	*689*	779	842	754	824	$360,000	$612,000	$260,000	$540,000
Louisiana	*419*	587	576	638	641	$672,000	$628,000	$876,000	$888,000
Maine	*329*	322	336	274	291	$0	$28,000	$0	$0
Maryland	*197*	210	606	637	514	$52,000	$36,000	$160,000	$0
Massachusetts	*794*	712	790	726	724	$0	$0	$0	$0
Michigan	*2,617*	2,731	3,089	2,597	2,500	$456,000	$1,888,000	$0	$0
Minnesota	*548*	768	652	619	566	$880,000	$416,000	$284,000	$72,000
Mississippi	*290*	272	292	352	350	$240,000	$8,000	$248,000	$240,000
Missouri	*896*	956	1,009	954	1,048	$240,000	$452,000	$232,000	$608,000
Montana	*245*	238	185	181	234	$0	$0	$0	$0
Nebraska	*483*	537	575	424	408	$216,000	$368,000	$0	$0
Nevada	*453*	459	527	635	806	$24,000	$296,000	$728,000	$1,412,000
New Hampshire	*141*	167	136	173	144	$104,000	$0	$128,000	$12,000
New Jersey	*1,561*	1,255	1,349	1,282	1,084	$0	$0	$0	$0
New Mexico	*355*	427	437	420	351	$288,000	$328,000	$260,000	$0
New York	*2,488*	2,394	2,398	2,205	2,214	$584,000	$0	$0	$0
North Carolina	*1,521*	1,667	1,622	1,494	1,377	$584,000	$404,000	$0	$0
North Dakota	*125*	144	82	138	113	$76,000	$0	$52,000	$0
Ohio	*1,710*	1,505	1,453	1,359	1,420	$0	$0	$0	$0
Oklahoma	*1,227*	1,463	1,496	1,569	1,226	$944,000	$1,076,000	$1,368,000	$0
Oregon	*1,016*	1,050	1,101	780	652	$136,000	$340,000	$0	$0
Pennsylvania	*1,916*	2,082	2,234	2,362	1,999	$664,000	$1,272,000	$1,784,000	$332,000
Rhode Island	*239*	258	273	184	201	$76,000	$136,000	$0	$0

Table D-1. (Continued)

State	Baseline Number of Foster child adoptions in FY2007	Number of Foster Child Adoptions Finalized in				Incentives Earned for Foster Child Adoptions Finalized in			
		FY2008	FY2009	FY2010	FY2011	FY2008	FY2009	FY2010	FY2011
South Carolina	431	525	513	529	588	$376,000	$328,000	$392,000	$628,000
South Dakota	160	173	165	131	156	$52,000	$20,000	$0	$0
Tennessee	1,214	1,098	1,001	972	772	$0	$0	$0	$0
Texas	4,022	4,530	4,988	4,709	4,718	$2,032,000	$3,864,000	$2,748,000	$2,784,000
Utah	450	541	510	572	569	$364,000	$240,000	$488,000	$476,000
Vermont	195	181	156	161	134	$0	$0	$0	$0
Virginia	668	595	633	645	748		$0	$0	$320,000
Washington	1,276	1,245	1,618	1,626	1,573	$0	$1,368,000	$1,400,000	$1,188,000
West Virginia	398	513	537	654	685	$460,000	$556,000	$1,024,000	$1,148,000
Wisconsin	656	624	725	690	644	$0	$276,000	$136,000	$0
Wyoming	72	82	69	69	73	$40,000	$0	$0	$4,000
Puerto Rico	143	133	179	98	42	$0	$144,000	$0	$0
TOTAL	*51,306*	*54,106*	*55,793*	*51,662*	*48,662*	*$16,076,00*	*$23,448,00*	*$18,912,000*	*$16,028,000*

Source: Table prepared by the Congressional Research Service based on earnings and award data received from HHS, Administration for Children and Families (ACF), Administration on Children, Youth, and Families (ACYF), Children's Bureau. Data shown for numbers of adoptions are as determined for the Adoption Incentives program and may differ somewhat from data reported elsewhere on adoptions with public child welfare agency involvement.

Note: For incentives earned in FY2009, FY2010 and FY2011, there were insufficient appropriations to pay the full bonus amounts earned at the time of the initial awards. Accordingly, for incentives earned in FY2009 and FY2010, states received a portion of their bonus amount at the time of the initial award (i.e., at the end of the fiscal year following the fiscal year in which the incentive was earned) and the remainder when sufficient funds were available (in the following fiscal year). For incentives earned for increases in the number of foster child adoptions finalized in FY2011, states received an initial, partial award in August 2012. However, assuming it follows past practice, HHS is expected to use Adoption Incentives funds appropriated for FY2013 to pay states the remaining incentive amounts for increases in foster child adoptions (up to the full amount shown in the final column of the table).

[a] As part of its comments in *Child Welfare Outcomes, FY2008-FY2011*, Illinois notes it has begun an improvement plan to address certain data concerns, including recent system changes leading to a miscount of adoptions.

Table D-2. Older Child (Age 9 or Above) Adoptions and Incentives Earned, FY2008-FY2011

Initial incentive awards are paid in the fiscal year following the year in which the incentive was earned

State	Baseline Number of older child adoptions in FY2007	Number of Older Child Adoptions Finalized in				Incentives Earned for Older Child Adoptions Finalized in			
		FY2008	FY2009	FY2010	FY2011	FY2008	FY2009	FY2010	FY2011
Alabama	115	136	186	220	108	$168,000	$568,000	$840,000	$0
Alaska	72	87	99	114	89	$120,000	$216,000	$336,000	$136,000
Arizona	345	388	392	536	557	$344,000	$376,000	$1,528,000	$1,696,000
Arkansas	102	116	147	135	137	$112,000	$360,000	$264,000	$280,000
California	1,646	1,734	1,555	1,293	1,060	$704,000	$0	$0	$0
Colorado	236	207	204	210	207	$0	$0	$0	$0
Connecticut	140	157	156	142	126	$136,000	$128,000	$16,000	$0
Delaware	24	18	31	14	26	$0	$56,000	$0	$16,000
District of Columbia	63	38	36	49	40	$0	$0	$0	$0
Florida	703	951	919	843	771	$1,984,000	$1,728,000	$1,120,000	$544,000
Georgia	356	356	405	370	320	$0	$392,000	$112,000	$0
Hawaii	48	66	63	53	65	$144,000	$120,000	$40,000	$136,000
Idaho	56	60	92	83	80	$32,000	$288,000	$216,000	$192,000
Illinois	336	358	358	302	145[a]	$176,000	$176,000	$0	$0

Table D-2. (Continued)

State	Baseline Number of older child adoptions in FY2007	Number of Older Child Adoptions Finalized in				Incentives Earned for Older Child Adoptions Finalized in			
		FY2008	FY2009	FY2010	FY2011	FY2008	FY2009	FY2010	FY2011
Indiana	383	458	433	367	432	$600,000	$400,000	$0	$392,000
Iowa	240	213	217	179	163	$0	$0	$0	$0
Kansas	205	214	208	168	224	$72,000	$24,000	$0	$152,000
Kentucky	209	247	290	293	275	$304,000	$648,000	$672,000	$528,000
Louisiana	96	117	103	140	137	$168,000	$56,000	$352,000	$328,000
Maine	113	93	83	62	63	$0	$0	$0	$0
Maryland	43	61	170	167	140	$144,000	$160,000	$136,000	$0
Massachusetts	189	125	137	141	149	$0	$0	$0	$0
Michigan	828	843	963	758	694	$120,000	$1,080,000	$0	$0
Minnesota	153	158	158	162	148	$40,000	$40,000	$72,000	$0
Mississippi	95	84	86	91	111	$0	$0	$0	$128,000
Missouri	286	317	292	291	261	$248,000	$48,000	$40,000	$0
Montana	70	61	49	46	75	$0	$0	$0	$40,000
Nebraska	141	150	139	104	100	$0	$0	$0	$0
Nevada	122	122	111	153	223	$0	$0	$248,000	$808,000
New Hampshire	43	55	50	59	38	$96,000	$56,000	$128,000	$0
New Jersey	375	311	361	366	279	$0	$0	$0	$0
New Mexico	118	127	156	119	130	$72,000	$304,000	$8,000	$96,000
New York	1,053	976	952	798	803	$0	$0	$0	$0
North Carolina	376	438	455	460	408	$496,000	$632,000	$672,000	$256,000
North Dakota	27	26	24	37	29	$0	$0	$80,000	$16,000
Ohio	541	454	396	325	403	$0	$0	$0	$0

State	Baseline Number of older child adoptions in FY2007	Number of Older Child Adoptions Finalized in				Incentives Earned for Older Child Adoptions Finalized in			
		FY2008	FY2009	FY2010	FY2011	FY2008	FY2009	FY2010	FY2011
Oklahoma	343	376	350	381	320	$264,000	$56,000	$304,000	$0
Oregon	234	227	250	154	133	$0	$128,000	$0	$0
Pennsylvania	538	516	501	554	459	$0	$0	$128,000	$0
Rhode Island	57	64	63	44	54	$56,000	$48,000	$0	$0
South Carolina	113	135	125	126	150	$176,000	$96,000	$104,000	$296,000
South Dakota	51	38	42	36	41	$0	$0	$0	$0
Tennessee	524	435	342	379	276	$0	$0	$0	$0
Texas	805	1,007	1,122	1,172	1,246	$1,616,000	$2,536,000	$2,936,000	$3,528,000
Utah	80	93	83	105	106	$104,000	$24,000	$200,000	$208,000
Vermont	67	50	50	54	37	$0	$0	$0	$0
Virginia	215	164	217	224	294	$0	$16,000	$72,000	$632,000
Washington	246	240	307	392	332	$0	$488,000	$1,168,000	$688,000
West Virginia	105	107	153	183	179	$16,000	$384,000	$624,000	$592,000
Wisconsin	219	175	187	178	152	$0	$0	$0	$0
Wyoming	12	23	19	18	20	$88,000	$56,000	$48,000	$64,000
Puerto Rico	34	36	70	28	11	$16,000	$288,000	$0	$0
TOTAL	13,591	14,008	14,357	13,678	12,826	$8,688,00	$11,976,000	$12,464,000	$11,752,000

Source: Table prepared by the Congressional Research Service based on earnings and award data received from HHS, Administration for Children and Families (ACF), Administration on Children, Youth, and Families (ACYF), Children's Bureau. Data shown for numbers of adoptions are as determined for the Adoption Incentives program and may differ somewhat from data reported elsewhere on adoptions with public child welfare agency involvement.

Note: For incentives earned in FY2009, FY2010 and FY2011, there were insufficient appropriations to pay the full bonus amounts earned at the time of the initial awards. Accordingly, for incentives earned in FY2009 and FY2010, states received a portion of their bonus amount at the time of the initial award (i.e., at the end of the fiscal year following the fiscal year in which the incentive was earned) and the remainder when sufficient funds were available (in the following fiscal year). For incentives earned for increases in the number of older child adoptions finalized in FY2011, states received an initial, partial award in August 2012. However, assuming it follows past practice, HHS is expected to use Adoption Incentives funds appropriated for FY2013 to pay states the remaining incentive amounts for increases in older child adoptions (up to the full amount shown in the final column of the table).

[a] As part of its comments in *Child Welfare Outcomes, FY2008-FY2011*, Illinois notes it has begun an improvement plan to address certain data concerns, including recent system changes leading to a miscount of adoptions.

Table D-3. Special Needs (Under Age 9) Adoptions and Incentives Earned, FY2008-FY2011

Initial incentive awards are paid in the fiscal year following the year in which the incentive was earned

State	Baseline Number of Special Needs (under 9) Adoptions in FY2007	Number of Special Needs (under age 9) Adoptions Finalized in				Incentives Earned for Special Needs (under age 9) Adoptions Finalized in			
		FY2008	FY2009	FY2010	FY2011	FY2008	FY2009	FY2010	FY2011
Alabama	110	118	20	6	58	$32,000	$0	$0	$0
Alaska	127	136	182	160	146	$36,000	$220,000	$132,000	$76,000
Arizona	1,026	989	973	1,180	1,388	$0	$0	$616,000	$1,448,000
Arkansas	181	256	285	320	289	$300,000	$416,000	$556,000	$432,000
California	4,921	4,884	4,539	3,735	3,248	$0	$0	$0	$0
Colorado	356	96	332	300	310	$0	$0	$0	$0
Connecticut	310	282	270	237	167	$0	$0	$0	$0
Delaware [a]	19	35	27	18	20	$0	$32,000	$0	$4,000
District of Columbia	52	38	12	0	44	$0	$0	$0	$0
Florida	1,181	1,994	1,570	1,589	1,543	$3,252,000	$1,556,000	$1,632,000	$1,448,000
Georgia	459	489	453	434	446	$120,000	$0	$0	$0

State	Baseline Number of Special Needs (under 9) Adoptions in FY2007	Number of Special Needs (under age 9) Adoptions Finalized in				Incentives Earned for Special Needs (under age 9) Adoptions Finalized in			
		FY2008	FY2009	FY2010	FY2011	FY2008	FY2009	FY2010	FY2011
Hawaii	170	164	161	116	96	$0	$0	$0	$0
Idaho	106	147	210	198	155	$164,000	$416,000	$368,000	$196,000
Illinois [a]	0	0	462	670	253 [b]	$0	$0	$0	$0
Indiana	708	601	623	809	675	$0	$0	$404,000	$0
Iowa [a]	399	424	384	299	346	$0	$232,000	$0	$0
Kansas	396	343	454	369	394	$0	$288,000	$0	$252,000
Kentucky	464	489	536	445	527	$100,000	$452,000	$0	$456,000
Louisiana	210	299	323	342	324	$356,000	$100,000	$528,000	$88,000
Maine [a]	137	154	162	143	159	$68,000	$0	$0	$0
Maryland	23	0	82	294	86	$0	$0	$0	$0
Massachusetts	320	205	268	209	220	$0	$0	$0	$0
Michigan	1,027	1,097	1,276	831	46	$280,000	$996,000	$0	$0
Minnesota	231	323	243	191	228	$368,000	$48,000	$0	$0
Mississippi	149	149	158	199	192	$0	$36,000	$200,000	$172,000
Missouri	521	398	540	571	646	$0	$76,000	$200,000	$500,000
Montana	142	139	91	83	81	$0	$0	$0	$0
Nebraska [a]	114	175	202	168	157	$244,000	$352,000	$360,000	$648,000
Nevada	288	285	346	378	450	$0	$232,000	$0	$0
New Hampshire	87	103	68	86	71	$64,000	$0	$0	$0
New Jersey	885	242	577	578	459	$0	$0	$0	$0
New Mexico	207	245	235	249	173	$152,000	$112,000	$168,000	$0
New York [a]	969	1,022	1,082	1,071	924	$0	$0	$0	$0
North Carolina	757	812	802	768	744	$220,000	$180,000	$44,000	$0
North Dakota	60	49	29	39	51	$0	$0	$0	$0

Table D-3. (Continued)

State	Baseline Number of Special Needs (under 9) Adoptions in FY2007	Number of Special Needs (under age 9) Adoptions Finalized in				Incentives Earned for Special Needs (under age 9) Adoptions Finalized in			
		FY2008	FY2009	FY2010	FY2011	FY2008	FY2009	FY2010	FY2011
Ohio	1,135	919	880	890	903	$0	$0	$0	$0
Oklahoma	609	683	666	649	548	$296,000	$228,000	$160,000	$0
Oregon	615	636	678	481	443	$84,000	$252,000	$0	$0
Pennsylvania	1,099	1,232	1,395	1,413	1,253	$532,000	$1,184,000	$1,256,000	$616,000
Rhode Island	118	137	128	81	102	$76,000	$40,000	$0	$0
South Carolina	163	198	242	181	241	$140,000	$316,000	$72,000	$312,000
South Dakota [a]	75	89	87	69	88	$56,000	$48,000	$0	$0
Tennessee [a]	196	334	311	249	282	$552,000	$0	$212,000	$0
Texas	2,214	2,471	2,722	2,566	2,617	$1,028,000	$2,032,000	$1,408,000	$1,612,000
Utah	149	229	205	174	193	$320,000	$224,000	$100,000	$176,000
Vermont [a]	85	88	51	80	56	$0	$0	$0	$0
Virginia	327	309	282	271	290	$0	$0	$0	$0
Washington	975	936	576	938	935	$0	$0	$0	$0
West Virginia	244	252	300	332	308	$32,000	$224,000	$352,000	$256,000
Wisconsin [a]	422	402	431	410	439	$0	$36,000	$0	$0
Wyoming	31	27	22	19	9	$0	$0	$0	$0
Puerto Rico	36	45	34	28	8	$36,000	$0	$0	$0
TOTAL	25,605	26,169	26,987	25,916	23,831	$8,908,000	$10,328,000	$8,768,000	$8,692,000

Source: Table prepared by the Congressional Research Service based on earnings and award data received from HHS, Administration for Children and Families (ACF), Administration on Children, Youth, and Families (ACYF), Children's Bureau. Data shown for numbers of adoptions are as determined for the Adoption Incentives program and may differ somewhat from data reported elsewhere on adoptions with public child welfare agency involvement.

Note: For incentives earned in FY2009, FY2010 and FY2011, there were insufficient appropriations to pay the full bonus amounts earned at the time of the initial awards. Accordingly, for incentives earned in FY2009 and FY2010, states received a portion of their bonus amount at the time of the initial award (i.e., at the end of the fiscal year following the fiscal year in which the incentive was earned) and the remainder when sufficient funds were available (in the following fiscal year). For incentives earned for increases in the number of special needs (under age 9) adoptions finalized in FY2011, states received an initial, partial award in August 2012. However, assuming it follows past practice, HHS is expected to use Adoption Incentives funds appropriated for FY2013 to pay states the remaining incentive amounts for increases in special needs (under age 9) adoptions (up to the full amount shown in the final column of the table).

a As provided in the law, states that exceeded their special needs (under age 9) adoption baseline did not earn an incentive for this increase unless, in that same fiscal year, they separately earned an incentive for increases in foster child or older child adoptions, or if they improved their adoption rate.

b As part of its comments in *Child Welfare Outcomes, FY2008-FY2011*, Illinois notes it has begun an improvement plan to address certain data concerns, including recent system changes leading to a miscount of adoptions.

Table D-4. Adoption Rates and Incentive Increases for Improved Adoption Rate
Adoption Rate = Number of foster child adoptions finalized in the fiscal year for every 100 children in foster care on the last day of the previous fiscal year

State	Initial Baseline: Highest adoption rate FY2002-F2007	Actual Adoption Rate Achieved				Current Baseline: Highest adoption rate FY2002-FY2011	Fiscal Year Highest Adoption Rate Achieved	Incentive Increases States Were Eligible to Receive			
		FY2008	FY2009	FY2010	FY2011			FY2008	FY2009	FY2010	FY2011
Alabama	6.5	5.5	9.1	9.8	8.2	9.8	FY2010	$0	$177,000	$44,000	$0
Alaska	12.3	12.3	15.6	15.5	16.5	16.5	FY2011	$0	$71,000	$0	$17,000
Arizona	16.0	16.7	15.7	21.7	22.6	22.6	FY2011	$65,000	$0	$471,000	$88,000
Arkansas	12.5	13.8	16.8	16.1	15.7	16.8	FY2009	$46,000	$105,000	$0	$0

Table D-4. (Continued)

State	Initial Baseline (Highest adoption rate FY2002-F2007)	Actual Adoption Rate Achieved				Current Baseline (Highest adoption rate FY2002-FY2011)	Fiscal Year Highest Adoption Rate Achieved	Incentive Increases States Were Eligible to Receive			
		FY2008	FY2009	FY2010	FY2011			FY2008	FY2009	FY2010	FY2011
California	10.0	10.5	10.4	9.4	8.9	10.5	FY2008	$377,000	$0	$0	$0
Colorado	13.2	12.8	13.3	13.1	13.3	13.3	FY2009	$0	$11,000	$0	$0
Connecticut	8.9	11.2	12.7	11.8	11.3	12.7	FY2009	$132,000	$82,000	$0	$0
Delaware	13.0	9.6	13.3	8.2	12.9	13.3	FY2009	$0	$3,000	$0	$0
District of Columbia	12.2	5.1	4.5	6.0	5.0	12.2	FY2004	$0	$0	$0	$0
Florida	10.4	14.8	17.0	16.9	15.5	17.0	FY2009	$1,173,000	$479,000	$0	$0
Georgia	9.4	10.4	12.4	14.8	15.4	15.4	FY2011	$118,000	$204,000	$193,000	$40,000
Hawaii	14.7	13.2	16.3	14.4	15.6	16.3	FY2009	$0	$27,000	$0	$0
Idaho	11.7	12.2	19.6	21.2	17.4	21.2	FY2010	$10,000	$128,000	$23,000	$0
Illinois	12.9	8.5	7.9	7.1	2.7^a	12.9	FY2002	$0	$0	$0	$0
Indiana	11.2	13.2	12.6	11.9	12.7	13.2	FY2008	$232,000	$0	$0	$0
Iowa	21.0	12.6	14.9	12.1	13.0	21.0	FY2003	$0	$0	$0	$0
Kansas	12.5	10.6	13.7	12.0	13.0	13.7	FY2009	$0	$75,000	$0	$0
Kentucky	12.5	11.1	11.7	11.0	11.8	12.5	FY2005	$0	$0	$0	$0
Louisiana	10.6	11.0	11.4	13.3	14.4	14.4	FY2011	$22,000	$19,000	$92,000	$49,000
Maine	15.8	16.3	18.0	16.6	18.8	18.8	FY2011	$11,000	$32,000	$0	$13,000
Maryland	7.3	2.1	7.8	9.0	8.4	9.0	FY2010	$0	$40,000	$86,000	$0
Massachusetts	7.2	6.8	7.6	7.5	8.1	8.1	FY2011	$0	$39,000	$0	$43,000

State							FY				
Michigan	13.6	13.1	15.3	14.7	15.2	15.3	FY2009	$0	$346,000	$0	$0
Minnesota	10.1	11.4	10.8	11.4	11.2	11.4	FY2008	$86,000	$0	$0	$0
Mississippi	9.9	8.2	8.9	10.6	9.8	10.6	FY2010	$0	$0	$23,000	$0
Missouri	11.1	9.7	10.0	11.1	10.6	11.1	FY2002	$0	$0	$0	$0
Montana	12.8	13.7	11.6	11.0	13.6	13.7	FY2008	$16,000	$66,000	$0	$0
Nebraska	7.8	9.1	10.3	7.9	7.6	10.3	FY2009	$79,000	$66,000	$0	$0
Nevada	9.8	9.1	10.5	13.3	16.8	16.8	FY2011	$0	$35,000	$133,000	$167,000
New Hampshire	12.3	15.4	13.2	18.6	17.2	18.6	FY2010	$34,000	$0	$30,000	$0
New Jersey	14.5	13.9	15.9	16.4	15.7	16.4	FY2010	$0	$115,000	$41,000	$0
New Mexico	15.7	17.6	19.7	21.1	18.8	21.1	FY2010	$47,000	$46,000	$28,000	$0
New York	10.8	8.0	8.1	7.9	8.3	10.8	FY2004	$0	$0	$0	$0
North Carolina	13.7	15.4	16.5	15.6	15.6	16.5	FY2009	$184,000	$106,000	$0	$0
North Dakota	10.7	11.4	6.6	11.4	10.5	11.4	FY2008	$9,000	$0	$0	$0
Ohio	11.2	8.8	10.6	11.1	11.9	11.9	FY2011	$0	$0	$0	$83,000
Oklahoma	12.9	12.4	14.1	18.0	15.6	18.0	FY2010	$0	$129,000	$341,000	$0
Oregon	12.4	11.0	12.2	9.0	7.2	12.4	FY2002	$0	$0	$0	$0
Pennsylvania	9.3	10.0	11.6	13.9	13.2	13.9	FY2010	$142,000	$312,000	$394,000	$0
Rhode Island	11.0	9.5	11.3	8.7	9.6	11.3	FY2009	$0	$8,000	$0	$0
South Carolina	9.0	10.2	10.3	10.7	13.1	13.1	FY2011	$62,000	$3,000	$20,000	$108,000
South Dakota	10.4	11.0	11.1	8.8	10.5	11.1	FY2009	$10,000	$2,000	$0	$0
Tennessee	14.1	14.2	13.9	14.5	11.5	14.5	FY2010	$5,000	$0	$17,000	$0
Texas	13.0	15.0	17.7	17.6	16.3	17.7	FY2009	$612,000	$765,000	$0	$0
Utah	21.6	19.8	18.8	20.7	19.7	21.6	FY2006	$0	$0	$0	$0
Vermont	15.0	13.8	13.0	15.2	14.4	15.2	FY2010	$0	$0	$2,000	$0
Virginia	8.7	8.0	8.9	10.9	13.8	13.8	FY2011	$0	$15,000	$117,000	$158,000
Washington	13.6	11.2	14.1	14.8	15.5	15.5	FY2011	$0	$53,000	$80,000	$73,000
West Virginia	10.9	11.6	12.2	15.4	16.7	16.7	FY2011	$32,000	$25,000	$137,000	$52,000

Table D-4. (Continued)

State	Initial Baseline *Highest adoption rate FY2002-F2007*	Actual Adoption Rate Achieved				Current Baseline *Highest adoption rate FY2002-FY2011*	Fiscal Year Highest Adoption Rate Achieved	Incentive Increases States Were Eligible to Receive				
		FY2008	FY2009	FY2010	FY2011			FY2008	FY2009	FY2010	FY2011	
Wisconsin	*14.3*	8.4	9.8	10.2	9.8	*14.3*	FY2004	$0	$0	$0	$0	
Wyoming	*6.1*	6.7	6.0	6.0	7.4	*7.4*	FY2011	$7,000	$0	$0	$7,000	
Puerto Rico	*2.7*	2.0	2.9	1.8	0.9	*2.9*	FY2009	$0	$12,000	$0	$0	
Median	*12.0*	11.2	12.2	12.0	13.1	*13.8*		$3,511,000	$3,530,000	$2,272,000	$898,000	

Source: Table prepared by the Congressional Research Service based on earnings and award data received from HHS, Administration for Children and Families, Administration on Children, Youth, and Families, Children's Bureau. Adoption data used to calculate these rates are based on foster child adoptions as counted for the Adoption Incentives program.

Note: A state is eligible for an increase in its Adoption Incentive award (above the amount, if any, it earned for increases in number of adoptions) if it improves its adoption rate. However, any increase due to improved adoption *rates* may only be paid if there are sufficient funds remaining after the awards are made for increased *numbers* of adoption. FY2008 is the first year for which increases tied to improved adoption rates were authorized and it is also the only earnings year for which some funds were available to pay these increases. Specifically, for that year there were sufficient funds to pay about one-half (48%) of the increases for which states with improved adoption rates were eligible. (The full increase for which states were eligible is shown in the table above, although states received less than $1.7 million of these amounts.) In each succeeding earnings year, there were no funds available to pay increased incentive amounts to states with improved adoption rates. Therefore, none of the amounts shown in the table above (for FY2009, FY2010, or FY2011) were paid to states that improved their adoption rates in those years.

[a] As part of its comments in *Child Welfare Outcomes, FY2008-FY2011*, Illinois notes it has begun an improvement plan to address certain data concerns, including recent system changes leading to a miscount of adoptions.

Table D-5. Incentives Earned by Award Category for Adoptions Finalized in FY2008-FY2011

Blank cell indicates not applicable

State	Foster Child $	%	Older Child $	%	Special Needs under Age 9 $	%	Adoption Rate $	%	Total Incentive Amount for which State was Eligible	Adoption Rate Amount Paid $	%	TOTAL Expected to Be Paida
Alabama	$2,700,000	59.6%	$1,576,000	34.8%	$32,000	0.7%	$221,000	4.9%	$4,529,000	$0	0.0%	$4,308,000
Alaska	$1,004,000	42.5%	$808,000	34.2%	$464,000	19.6%	$88,000	3.7%	$2,364,000	$0	0.0%	$2,276,000
Arizona	$5,040,000	43.2%	$3,944,000	33.8%	$2,064,000	17.7%	$624,000	5.3%	$11,672,000	$31,200	5.0%	$11,079,200
Arkansas	$2,652,000	48.0%	$1,016,000	18.4%	$1,704,000	30.9%	$151,000	2.7%	$5,523,000	$22,080	14.6%	$5,394,080
California	$620,000	36.4%	$704,000	41.4%	$0	0.0%	$377,000	22.2%	$1,701,000	$180,960	48.0%	$1,504,960
Colorado	$0	0.0%	$0	0.0%	$0	0.0%	$11,000	100.0%	$11,000	$0	0.0%	$0
Connecticut	$772,000	61.0%	$280,000	22.1%	$0	0.0%	$214,000	16.9%	$1,266,000	$63,360	29.6%	$1,115,360
Delaware	$28,000	20.1%	$72,000	51.8%	$36,000	25.9%	$3,000	2.2%	$139,000	$0	0.0%	$136,000
District of Columbia	$0		$0		$0		$0		$0			$0
Florida	$8,220,000	35.5%	$5,376,000	23.2%	$7,888,000	34.1%	$1,652,000	7.1%	$23,136,000	$563,040	34.1%	$22,047,040
Georgia	$132,000	10.1%	$504,000	38.4%	$120,000	9.2%	$555,000	42.3%	$1,311,000	$56,640	10.2%	$812,640
Hawaii	$152,000	24.6%	$440,000	71.1%	$0	0.0%	$27,000	4.4%	$619,000	$0	0.0%	$592,000
Idaho	$1,468,000	41.9%	$728,000	20.8%	$1,144,000	32.7%	$161,000	4.6%	$3,501,000	$4,800	3.0%	$3,344,800
Illinois	$60,000	14.6%	$352,000	85.4%	$0	0.0%	$0	0.0%	$412,000	$0	0.0%	$412,000
Indiana	$3,872,000	65.6%	$1,392,000	23.6%	$404,000	6.8%	$232,000	3.9%	$5,900,000	$111,360	48.0%	$5,779,360
Iowa	$0		$0		$0		$0		$0			$0
Kansas	$344,000	38.3%	$248,000	27.6%	$232,000	25.8%	$75,000	8.3%	$899,000	$0	0.0%	$824,000
Kentucky	$1,772,000	38.8%	$2,152,000	47.2%	$640,000	14.0%	$0	0.0%	$4,564,000	$0		$4,564,000
Louisiana	$3,064,000	51.6%	$904,000	15.2%	$1,792,000	30.2%	$182,000	3.1%	$5,942,000	$10,560	5.8%	$5,770,560
Maine	$28,000	8.2%	$0	0.0%	$256,000	75.3%	$56,000	16.5%	$340,000	$5,280	9.4%	$289,280
Maryland	$248,000	30.5%	$440,000	54.1%	$0	0.0%	$126,000	15.5%	$814,000	$0	0.0%	$688,000
Massachusetts	$0	0.0%	$0	0.0%	$0	0.0%	$82,000	100.0%	$82,000	$0	0.0%	$0
Michigan	$2,344,000	45.4%	$1,200,000	23.2%	$1,276,000	24.7%	$346,000	6.7%	$5,166,000	$0	0.0%	$4,820,000
Minnesota	$1,652,000	71.6%	$152,000	6.6%	$416,000	18.0%	$86,000	3.7%	$2,306,000	$41,280	48.0%	$2,261,280

Table D-5. (Continued)

State	Foster Child $	%	Older Child $	%	Special Needs under Age 9 $	%	Adoption Rate $	%	Total Incentive Amount for which State was Eligible	Adoption Rate Amount Paid $	%	TOTAL Expected to Be Paid
Mississippi	$496,000	47.0%	$128,000	12.1%	$408,000	38.7%	$23,000	2.2%	$1,055,000	$0	0.0%	$1,032,000
Missouri	$1,532,000	57.9%	$336,000	12.7%	$776,000	29.3%	$0	0.0%	$2,644,000			$2,644,000
Montana	$0	0.0%	$40,000	71.4%	$0	0.0%	$16,000	28.6%	$56,000	$7,680	48.0%	$47,680
Nebraska	$584,000	41.8%	$72,000	5.2%	$596,000	42.7%	$145,000	10.4%	$1,397,000	$37,920	26.2%	$1,289,920
Nevada	$2,460,000	48.3%	$1,056,000	20.7%	$1,240,000	24.4%	$335,000	6.6%	$5,091,000	$0	0.0%	$4,756,000
New Hampshire	$244,000	37.4%	$280,000	42.9%	$64,000	9.8%	$64,000	9.8%	$652,000	$16,320	25.5%	$604,320
New Jersey	$0	0.0%	$0	0.0%	$0	0.0%	$156,000	100.0%	$156,000	$0	0.0%	$0
New Mexico	$876,000	45.9%	$480,000	25.1%	$432,000	22.6%	$121,000	6.3%	$1,909,000	$22,560	18.6%	$1,810,560
New York	$0		$0		$0		$0		$0			$0
North Carolina	$988,000	26.2%	$2,056,000	54.4%	$444,000	11.8%	$290,000	7.7%	$3,778,000	$88,320	30.5%	$3,576,320
North Dakota	$128,000	54.9%	$96,000	41.2%	$0	0.0%	$9,000	3.9%	$233,000	$4,320	48.0%	$228,320
Ohio	$0	0.0%	$0	0.0%	$0	0.0%	$83,000	100.0%	$83,000	$0	0.0%	$0
Oklahoma	$3,388,000	65.6%	$624,000	12.1%	$684,000	13.2%	$470,000	9.1%	$5,166,000	$0	0.0%	$4,696,000
Oregon	$476,000	50.6%	$128,000	13.6%	$336,000	35.7%	$0	0.0%	$940,000			$940,000
Pennsylvania	$4,052,000	47.0%	$128,000	1.5%	$3,588,000	41.6%	$848,000	9.8%	$8,616,000	$68,160	8.0%	$7,836,160
Rhode Island	$212,000	48.2%	$104,000	23.6%	$116,000	26.4%	$8,000	1.8%	$440,000	$0	0.0%	$432,000
South Carolina	$1,724,000	50.3%	$672,000	19.6%	$840,000	24.5%	$193,000	5.6%	$3,429,000	$29,760	15.4%	$3,265,760
South Dakota	$72,000	38.3%	$0	0.0%	$104,000	55.3%	$12,000	6.4%	$188,000	$4,800	40.0%	$180,800
Tennessee	$0	0.0%	$0	0.0%	$764,000	97.2%	$22,000	2.8%	$786,000	$2,400	10.9%	$766,400
Texas	$11,428,000	38.7%	$10,616,000	36.0%	$6,080,000	20.6%	$1,377,000	4.7%	$29,501,000	$293,760	21.3%	$28,417,760
Utah	$1,568,000	53.6%	$536,000	18.3%	$820,000	28.0%	$0	0.0%	$2,924,000			$2,924,000
Vermont	$0	0.0%	$0	0.0%	$0	0.0%	$2,000	100.0%	$2,000	$0	0.0%	$0
Virginia	$320,000	24.1%	$720,000	54.1%	$0	0.0%	$290,000	21.8%	$1,330,000	$0	0.0%	$1,040,000
Washington	$3,956,000	60.8%	$2,344,000	36.0%	$0	0.0%	$206,000	3.2%	$6,506,000	$0	0.0%	$6,300,000
West Virginia	$3,188,000	53.9%	$1,616,000	27.3%	$864,000	14.6%	$246,000	4.2%	$5,914,000	$15,360	6.2%	$5,683,360

State	Foster Child		Older Child		Special Needs under Age 9		Adoption Rate		Total Incentive Amount for which State was Eligible	Adoption Rate Amount Paid		TOTAL Expected to Be Paid[a]
	$	%	$	%	$	%	$	%		$	%	$
Wisconsin	$412,000	92.0%	$0	0.0%	$36,000	8.0%	$0	0.0%	$448,000			$448,000
Wyoming	$44,000	14.0%	$256,000	81.5%	$0	0.0%	$14,000	4.5%	$314,000	$3,360	24.0%	$303,360
Puerto Rico	$144,000	29.0%	$304,000	61.3%	$36,000	7.3%	$12,000	2.4%	$496,000	$0	0.0%	$484,000
TOTAL	$74,464,000	44.8%	$44,880,000	27.0%	$36,696,000	22.1%	$10,211,000	6.1%	$166,251,000	$1,685,280	16.5%	$157,725,280

Source: Table prepared by the Congressional Research Service based on earnings and award data received from HHS, Administration for Children and Families (ACF), Administration on Children, Youth, and Families (ACYF), Children's Bureau.

Note: States are expected to receive all incentive amounts they were eligible to receive for increases in the number of foster child, older child, and special needs (under age 9) adoptions. However, they may only receive awards for improved adoption rates if there are sufficient funds to pay these awards at the time initial awards are made for a fiscal year and *after* all awards for increases in numbers of adoptions are made. There were sufficient funds to pay some (48%) of awards earned for improved adoption rates for adoptions finalized in FY2008. However, there were no funds for this award category for adoptions finalized in FY2009, FY2010, or FY2011.

[a] In August 2012, states received an initial portion of any incentive earned for increases in the number of foster child, older child, or special needs (under age 9) adoptions. At that time there were insufficient funds to pay the full amount states earned. Therefore, states received a pro-rated amount ($31.8 million, 87%) of the award they were eligible for increases in numbers of adoptions. Assuming HHS follows past practice, however, states are expected to receive the remaining award amount ($4.7 million) out of FY2013 appropriations provided for the Adoption Incentive program.

APPENDIX E. CHILDREN IN FOSTER CARE AND WAITING FOR ADOPTION BY STATE

Table E-1. Children in Foster Care on the Last Day of the Fiscal Year by State, FY2007-FY2011 States are ordered by caseload change (largest % decline to greatest % increase), FY2007 to FY2011

State	FY2007	FY2008	FY2009	FY2010	FY2011	% Change in Caseload FY2007-FY2011
Hawaii	1,940	1,621	1,472	1,234	1,126	-42.0%
Georgia	12,197	9,984	8,068	6,895	7,591	-37.8%
Virginia	7,718	7,099	5,968	5,414	4,846	-37.2%
Rhode Island	2,768	2,407	2,112	2,086	1,806	-34.8%
Maine	1,971	1,864	1,646	1,546	1,296	-34.2%
New Hampshire	1,102	1,029	930	839	742	-32.7%
Pennsylvania	20,999	26,571	16,623	15,179	14,175	-32.5%
Maryland	8,415	7,613	7,065	6,098	5,704	-32.2%
Puerto Rico	6,330	6,185	5,351	4,476	4,363	-31.1%
Oklahoma	11,785	10,595	8,712	7,857	8,280	-29.7%
New Jersey	9,056	8,510	7,803	6,892	6,440	-28.9%
Wyoming	1,231	1,154	1,155	981	886	-28.0%
Idaho	1,870	1,723	1,446	1,462	1,354	-27.6%
Michigan	20,830	20,171	17,723	16,412	15,105	-27.5%
Alabama	7,262	6,941	6,179	5,350	5,295	-27.1%
Delaware	1,157	938	814	739	845	-27.0%
Florida	26,788	22,187	19,162	18,743	19,760	-26.2%
South Carolina	5,167	5,054	4,978	4,487	3,821	-26.0%
Minnesota	6,711	6,028	5,410	5,050	4,995	-25.6%
California	73,998	67,703	60,583	56,183	55,409	-25.1%
New Mexico	2,423	2,221	1,992	1,869	1,859	-23.3%
Vermont	1,309	1,200	1,062	933	1,010	-22.8%
Iowa	8,005	6,743	6,564	6,533	6,344	-20.7%
North Carolina	10,827	9,841	9,547	8,828	8,601	-20.6%
District of Columbia	2,197	2,217	2,111	2,066	1,797	-18.2%
Massachusetts	10,497	10,427	9,652	8,958	8,619	-17.9%
New York	30,072	29,493	27,992	26,783	24,962	-17.0%

State	FY2007	FY2008	FY2009	FY2010	FY2011	% Change in Caseload FY2007-FY2011
Ohio	14,532	13,703	12,232	11,940	12,069	-16.9%
Colorado	7,777	7,964	7,392	6,980	6,488	-16.6%
North Dakota	1,263	1,223	1,210	1,078	1,066	-15.6%
Louisiana	5,333	5,065	4,786	4,453	4,531	-15.0%
Connecticut	5,764	5,373	4,761	4,462	4,926	-14.5%
Washington	11,107	11,167	10,961	10,136	9,533	-14.2%
Alaska	2,126	1,954	1,851	1,765	1,829	-14.0%
Wisconsin	7,541	7,403	6,785	6,575	6,547	-13.2%
Nebraska	5,875	5,591	5,343	5,358	5,117	-12.9%
Kansas	6,631	6,306	5,691	5,979	5,852	-11.7%
South Dakota	1,566	1,482	1,484	1,485	1,407	-10.2%
Nevada	5,070	5,023	4,783	4,807	4,636	-8.6%
Kentucky	7,207	7,182	6,872	6,983	6,659	-7.6%
Oregon	9,562	8,988	8,650	9,001	8,871	-7.2%
Indiana	11,295	11,903	12,238	12,276	10,779	-4.6%
Utah	2,765	2,714	2,759	2,886	2,701	-2.3%
Tennessee	7,751	7,219	6,723	6,695	7,647	-1.3%
Illinois	17,864	17,843	17,080	17,730	17,641	-1.2%
Texas	30,137	28,154	26,686	28,947	30,109	-0.1%
West Virginia	4,432	4,412	4,237	4,112	4,475	1.0%
Arkansas	3,616	3,522	3,657	3,756	3,732	3.2%
Montana	1,737	1,600	1,639	1,723	1,794	3.3%
Missouri	10,282	7,607	8,667	9,880	10,620	3.3%
Mississippi	3,328	3,292	3,320	3,582	3,597	8.1%
Arizona	9,099	9,590	9,423	9,930	10,883	19.6%
TOTAL	*488,285*	*463,799*	*421,350*	*406,412*	*400,540*	*-18.0%*

Source: Table prepared by the Congressional Research Service based on caseload data by state, included in HHS, ACF, ACYF, Children's Bureau, "Foster Care FY2003-FY2011: Entries, Exits and Number of Children in Care on the Last Day of Each Fiscal Year by State" (data are as reported by states via AFCARS as of July 2012).

Table E-2. Children Waiting for Adoption, FY2007-FY2011, Percentage Change in the Number of Those Children and Share Adopted by State States are ordered by change in number of waiting children (largest % decline to greatest % increase), FY2007-FY2011

State	Number of Children Waiting to be Adopted					% Change in Number of Waiting Children	Share of Children Waiting on Last Day of Previous Fiscal Year Who Were Adopted in	
	FY2007	FY2008	FY2009	FY2010	FY2011		FY2008	FY2011
Hawaii	733	555	428	351	277	-62.2%	49.2%	56.4%
Maryland	1,660	1,506	1,221	883	719	-56.7%	36.7%	60.0%
New Hampshire	325	297	272	227	167	-48.6%	51.4%	63.4%
Idaho	593	576	498	389	334	-43.7%	39.8%	66.6%
Minnesota	1,674	1,393	1,227	1,073	955	-43.0%	46.9%	54.1%
Illinois	5,598	4,608	2,728	2,944	3,272	-41.6%	26.3%	41.3%
Pennsylvania	3,408	3,525	2,943	2,551	2,045	-40.0%	61.3%	78.9%
California	20,830	17,847	15,664	14,872	12,881	-38.2%	37.3%	36.0%
Colorado	1,762	1,897	1,506	1,246	1,098	-37.7%	57.0%	75.0%
Florida	7,927	7,942	6,364	5,022	4,994	-37.0%	48.8%	58.6%
District of Columbia	560	493	486	419	357	-36.3%	20.2%	25.3%
Puerto Rico	1,145	1,071	956	903	746	-34.8%	13.3%	6.2%
Oregon	2,527	2,206	1,840	1,827	1,663	-34.2%	41.6%	36.0%
Rhode Island	400	415	333	310	267	-33.3%	65.0%	64.8%
Missouri	2,853	1,792	1,982	1,952	1,946	-31.8%	30.6%	61.4%
North Dakota	337	288	298	227	230	-31.8%	47.2%	52.4%
Michigan	6,115	5,674	4,902	5,236	4,237	-30.7%	44.7%	47.7%
New Jersey	3,262	3,009	2,694	2,464	2,294	-29.7%	38.8%	44.2%
Alabama	1,824	1,751	1,475	1,271	1,296	-28.9%	24.2%	34.6%
North Carolina	3,095	2,903	2,722	2,427	2,234	-27.8%	54.7%	60.3%
Georgia	2,162	2,244	1,802	1,690	1,567	-27.5%	62.0%	63.4%
Oklahoma	4,022	3,766	3,429	2,872	2,956	-26.5%	37.7%	45.1%
Ohio	3,762	3,477	3,380	3,013	2,789	-25.9%	43.5%	47.1%
Virginia	1,834	1,769	1,617	1,562	1,372	-25.2%	36.2%	48.3%
Vermont	257	225	231	180	196	-23.7%	70.8%	74.4%
Montana	597	521	537	495	460	-22.9%	40.5%	48.1%
Delaware	311	304	239	253	244	-21.5%	35.7%	37.5%
South Carolina	1,781	1,823	1,862	1,699	1,415	-20.6%	29.5%	34.6%
New Mexico	963	907	870	777	786	-18.4%	44.3%	45.2%
South Dakota	452	423	380	418	376	-16.8%	38.9%	40.2%
Maine	614	619	571	575	511	-16.8%	52.4%	51.5%
Iowa	1,299	1,158	1,003	1,068	1,088	-16.2%	80.1%	80.9%
New York	7,659	7,014	6,890	6,603	6,418	-16.2%	31.3%	33.5%
Wyoming	151	98	73	85	127	-15.9%	61.6%	85.9%
Kentucky	2,153	2,101	2,048	1,951	1,918	-10.9%	35.9%	42.2%
Indiana	3,210	3,090	3,224	3,192	2,886	-10.1%	46.8%	48.7%

State	Number of Children Waiting to be Adopted					% Change in Number of Waiting Children	Share of Children Waiting on Last Day of Previous Fiscal Year Who Were Adopted in	
	FY2007	FY2008	FY2009	FY2010	FY2011		FY2008	FY2011
Wisconsin	1,284	1,329	1,255	1,159	1,163	-9.4%	56.2%	61.9%
Massachusetts	2,868	2,846	2,839	2,758	2,672	-6.8%	24.8%	26.3%
Alaska	766	769	714	686	714	-6.8%	38.4%	42.9%
Mississippi	898	996	975	843	880	-2.0%	31.3%	42.5%
Washington	2,837	3,035	3,147	3,089	2,783	-1.9%	44.4%	51.2%
Utah	574	553	565	553	567	-1.2%	93.4%	104.3%
Texas	13,552	13,414	12,844	13,108	13,481	-0.5%	33.4%	36.0%
Kansas	1,812	1,960	1,852	1,825	1,817	0.3%	39.8%	42.8%
Nevada	1,936	2,200	2,098	2,094	1,968	1.7%	24.3%	39.2%
Louisiana	1,137	1,069	1,093	1,091	1,162	2.2%	52.4%	58.8%
Nebraska	805	881	831	768	831	3.2%	64.6%	53.8%
Arizona	2,516	2,323	2,792	2,673	2,822	12.2%	67.4%	85.1%
West Virginia	1,278	1,300	1,220	1,241	1,473	15.3%	40.9%	56.2%
Connecticut	1,162	1,430	1,354	1,245	1,341	15.4%	66.4%	49.1%
Tennessee	1,622	1,477	1,326	1,692	2,027	25.0%	64.5%	45.6%
Arkansas	780	872	850	1,604	1,414	81.3%	64.7%	36.8%
TOTAL	*133,682*	*125,741*	*114,450*	*109,456*	*104,236*	*-22.0%*	*41.3%*	*46.2%*

Source: Table prepared by the Congressional Research Service based on state-level data reported via AFCARS as of July 2012, included in HHS, ACF, ACYF, Children's Bureau, "Children in Public Foster Care Waiting to be Adopted" and "Adoptions of Children with Public Child Welfare Agency Involvement."

Notes: There is no definition in federal law or regulation for the term "waiting for adoption." For purposes of analysis, and as used in this table, the HHS, Children's Bureau counts as "waiting" any child in foster care with a case plan goal of adoption and/or to whom all parental rights have been terminated. However, it excludes from this count any youth 16 or older to whom all parental rights have been terminated if that youth has a case plan goal of "emancipation."

Although not true for every child, the very large majority of children adopted with public child welfare agency involvement were previously in foster care.

End Notes

[1] See "Conditions or Factors Used by States in Determining Special Needs," in CRS Report R42792, Child Welfare: A Detailed Overview of Program Eligibility and Funding for Foster Care, Adoption Assistance and Kinship Guardianship Assistance under Title IV-E of the Social Security Act, by Emilie Stoltzfus.

[2] CRS Report RL30759, Child Welfare: Implementation of the Adoption and Safe Families Act (P.L. 105-89), by Karen Spar.

3 In 2008, as part of the Fostering Connections to Success and Increasing Adoptions Act (P.L. 110-351) Congress expanded eligibility for Title IV-E adoption assistance by removing income criteria tied to the family from which a child had been removed (usually this is the child's biological family). The revised eligibility criteria are being phased in and now apply to only some children determined to have special needs. However, as of FY2018, any child determined by a state to have special needs may be eligible for ongoing, federally supported adoption assistance. See CRS Report RL34704, Child Welfare: The Fostering Connections to Success and Increasing Adoptions Act of 2008 (P.L. 110-351), by Emilie Stoltzfus and "Federal Adoption Assistance Eligibility Criteria" in CRS Report R42792, Child Welfare: A Detailed Overview of Program Eligibility and Funding for Foster Care, Adoption Assistance and Kinship Guardianship Assistance under Title IV-E of the Social Security Act, by Emilie Stoltzfus.

4 Adoptions are generally a matter of state law and most termination of parental rights (TPR) proceedings and adoption finalizations occur in state courts (although they may also occur in tribal courts). While TPR is required for nearly all adoptions, a few states (and certain tribes) recognize "tribal customary adoptions," which do not require TPR.

5 From the late FY1990s through FY2005, the annual number of children entering foster care remained fairly stable even as the national foster care caseload declined. This was due to more, and faster, exits of children from foster care via adoption (and to some extent guardianship). From FY2006 through FY2011, the continued decline of the national caseload has been driven by both a decline in the number of children entering foster care each year, as well as a continuation of relatively high numbers of exits to adoptions.

6 The most common case plan goal for children in foster care is to reunite with their parents. Smaller numbers of children in care have a case plan goal of living with another relative or living with a legal (relative or non-relative) guardian. Aside from these goals (and adoption), each of which plan for a child's exit from care to a permanent family, some youth in care have a goal of "emancipation" (leaving care as an "independent" adult) and others are assigned the goal of "long-term foster care." See HHS, ACF, ACYF, Children's Bureau, The AFCARS Report, No. 19 (July 2012).

7 For a more complete definition of "waiting children" see Glossary of Terms in Appendix A.

8 See "Prevent Entry or Reunite Children with Their Parents" in CRS Report R42794, Child Welfare: State Plan Requirements under the Title IV-E Foster Care, Adoption Assistance, and Kinship Guardianship Assistance Program , by Emilie Stoltzfus.

9 Ibid. See "Ensure Timely Placement in a New Permanent Family When Appropriate."

10 TPR must be determined for each parent individually. For more information see Child Welfare Information Gateway, State Statutes Series, Grounds for Involuntary Termination of Parental Rights (2010).

11 The Adoption Incentive program seeks to influence state child welfare agency behavior. Congress has, separately provided a tax credit to individuals who adopt children, including children with special needs. This "incentive" to adopt is not a part of the discussion in this report. However, for more information see, CRS Report RL33633, Tax Benefits for Families: Adoption, by Christine Scott.

12 These awards are separately calculated. One child's adoption (if child is age 9 or older) may be counted for purposes of determining awards in both categories. However, a state that increases its foster child adoptions does not necessarily increase its older child adoptions (or vice versa). To earn awards in both categories, the state must show increases in both categories.

[13] An award for an improved rate is calculated by multiplying the state's baseline adoption rate (i.e., highest rate achieved in FY2002 or any subsequent year preceding year for which award is being determined) by the number of children in the state's foster care caseload on the last day of the fiscal year preceding the year for which the award is being determined. This result is then subtracted from the number of foster child adoptions in the state in the year for which the award is being determined. The difference represents the number of adoptions that are attributed to the increased adoption rate and this number (rounded to nearest whole number) is multiplied by $1,000 to determine the award amount. For an example of this award calculation see HHS, ACF, Information Memorandum, "Adoption Incentive Payments," September 1, 2009 (ACYF-CB-IM-09-03), p. 6.

[14] Section 473A(b)(1) of the Social Security Act. Tribes may not participate in this program. See HHS, ACF, ACYFCB-IM-09-03, p. 1.

[15] Section 473A(b)(3) and (4) of the Social Security Act.

[16] Since its establishment, Section 473A(h)(2) has provided that funds appropriated for the Adoption Incentives program may be used in any fiscal year through the last fiscal year for which funding for the program is authorized (initially this was FY2003, then FY2008, and currently it is FY2013). However, the use of funds across years has usually been limited to fewer years due to language in the annual appropriations bill accompanying the program's funding.

[17] Section 473A(d)(3) of the Social Security Act. See also HHS, ACF, ACYF-CB-IM-09-03, September 1, 2009.

[18] Section 473A(d)(3) of the Social Security Act.

[19] For purposes of this discussion "states" are defined to include the 50 states, the District of Columbia and Puerto Rico, which makes a total of 52 states.

[20] Section 473A(e) of the Social Security Act. The 2008 reauthorization amended the law to ensure that states have a full two years from the date they receive the bonus funds to spend them. Prior law permitted states to spend funds through the end of the fiscal year following the fiscal year in which awards were made. However, because the bulk of award funding is provided in the waning days of the fiscal year, this typically permitted states only a little more than 12 months to spend the award funds.

[21] Section 473A(f) of the Social Security Act.

[22] Based on CRS review of state Annual Progress and Services Reports (APSRs) submitted by states, generally, in mid-to late-2012, as part of requesting certain federal FY2013 child welfare funding.

[23] See CRS Report R40218, Youth Transitioning from Foster Care: Issues for Congress, by Adrienne L. FernandesAlcantara.

[24] There is no formal definition in federal law or regulation of children who are "waiting for adoption." In its published counts of children "waiting for adoption," HHS counts any child in foster care who has a case plan goal of adoption and/or (in most cases) children for whom all parental rights have been terminated. Youth who are age 16 or older and for whom all parental rights have been terminated are excluded from this count if they have a case plan goal of "emancipation."

[25] U.S. Department of Health and Human Services (HHS), Administration for Children and Families (ACF), FY2014 Justification of Estimates for Appropriations Committees, April 2013, p. 152.

[26] See Opening Statement of Chairman Dave Reichert, Subcommittee on Human Resources of the House Ways and Means Committee, Hearing on Increasing Adoptions from Foster Care, February 27, 2013. (Hereafter Hearing, February 27, 2013.)

[27] Testimony of Rita Soronen, President and CEO, Dave Thomas Foundation for Adoption and Testimony of Pat O'Brien, Executive Director and Founder, You Gotta Believe! The Older Child Adoption and Permanency Movement, Inc., Hearing, February 27, 2013.

[28] Karin Malm, Sharon Vandivere, with Tiffany Allen, Kerry DeVooght, Raquel. Ellis, Amy McLindon, Jacqueline Smollar, Eric Williams, and Andrew Zinn, Evaluation Report Summary: The Wendy's Wonderful Kids' Initiative, Child Trends, Washington, D.C.: 2011, pp. 9-11, 14-15.

[29] Testimony of Rita Soronen, Hearing, February 27, 2013.

[30] Testimony of Kelly Rosati, Vice President, Community Outreach, Focus on the Family, Hearing, February 27, 2013.

[31] Ibid. See also Testimony of Nicole Dobbins, Executive Director, Voice for Adoption, Hearing, February 27, 2013.

[32] Testimony of Nicole Dobbins. Dobbins also sought more accountability from states on their use of projected savings from the growing federal investment in Title IV-E adoption assistance (authorized by the Fostering Connections to Success and Increasing Adoptions Act, P.L. 110-351). She maintained that states should be required to invest a portion of any savings they experience (due to this increased federal adoption assistance support) in post-adoption support services.

[33] Testimony of Rosati, including response to questions at Hearing, February 27, 2013. While states may make certain benefits available only to youth who remain in care, Congress has provided that certain education benefits and other assistance available to youth who "age out" of care (under Title IV-E of the Social Security Act) may also be available to youth who leave foster care for adoption or guardianship on or after their 16th birthday. In addition, as part of the Higher Education Act, Congress permits any youth who was in foster care on or after his/her 13th birthday to apply for federal financial aid as an "independent" student. For more information, see CRS Report RL34499, Youth Transitioning from Foster Care: Background and Federal Programs, by Adrienne L. Fernandes-Alcantara.

[34] Testimony of Nicole Dobbins, Executive Director, Voice for Adoption and Testimony of Pat O'Brien, Hearing, February 27, 2013.

[35] Testimony of Pat O'Brien, Hearing, February 27, 2013.

[36] Family Connection grants were established in the Fostering Connections to Success and Increasing Adoptions Act (P.L. 110-351). That law placed the grant program in Section 427 of the Social Security Act and appropriated five years of funding for them ($15 million annually for FY2009-FY2013). In addition to family group decision-making meetings, intensive family-finding efforts, and kinship navigator programs, these competitive grants have also been available for support of residential family treatment. For more information see "Family Connection Grantees" on the website of the HHS, Children's Bureau-supported National Resource Center for Permanency and Family Connections.

[37] The President's FY2014 budget calls for extension of this grant program for two years (FY2014-FY2016). It also proposes integrating the use of trauma-informed and trauma-focused approaches and or services (into the existing program focus areas) and increasing access to services for children subject to the Indian Child Welfare Act (ICWA). HHS, ACF FY2014 Justification of Estimates for Appropriations Committees, April 2013, p. 341.

[38] Testimony of Nicole Dobbins, Hearing, February 27, 2013.

[39] See response of each witness to question raised by Representative Danny Davis, Hearing, February 27, 2013.

In: The Adoption Incentives Program　　　　ISBN: 978-1-62948-758-8
Editors: Patrick L. Cales　　　　　　　© 2014 Nova Science Publishers, Inc.

Chapter 2

TESTIMONY OF NICOLE DOBBINS, EXECUTIVE DIRECTOR, VOICE FOR ADOPTION. HEARING ON "INCREASING ADOPTIONS FROM FOSTER CARE"[*]

Hello, Chairman Dave Reichert, Ranking Member Lloyd Doggett and members of the Subcommittee on Human Resources. I am Nicole Dobbins, Executive Director of Voice for Adoption (VFA). I am pleased to appear before you today to provide testimony regarding the importance of increasing adoptions for children in our nation's foster care system who are awaiting permanent families. Thank you for having this significant hearing and thank you for the opportunity to be a part of this distinguished panel.

Let me start by saying Voice for Adoption[1] is a membership advocacy organization. We speak out for our nation's 104,000 waiting children in foster care and the families that adopt children with special needs. VFA members, who are spread across the country, recruit families to adopt children and youth in foster care who are waiting for a permanent family. Our members also provide vital support services both before and after adoption finalization to help adoptive families through the challenges they sometimes face in parenting children who have experienced abuse or neglect. VFA members are dedicated to finding permanent, loving families for every waiting child in foster care. We

---

[*] This is an edited, reformatted and augmented version of a testimony, Presented February 27, 2013 before the House Committee on Ways and Means, Subcommittee on Human Resources.

are also committed to ensuring federal policies and funding match the ongoing needs of these children and their adoptive families.

I would like to shed light on four key areas within my allotted five minutes:

1. The rate of adoption from foster care is increasing, but the adoption of older youth continues to be a struggle for States.
2. Youth who "age-out" are a vulnerable population and more must be done to secure permanency for these youth before exiting foster care.
3. Adoption experts—both professionals and families alike—identify post-adoption services as a critical need to support families, but a lack of resources to support these efforts is still a challenge.
4. State accountability for the use of federal adoption funding should be reviewed to ensure that reinvestment into supporting adopted children and their families' is happening as required by law.

Overall, there have been great improvements since the federal government placed an emphasis on the importance of timelier adoptions of children from foster care when the *Adoption and Safe Families Act* (ASFA) of 1997 (P.L. 105-89) was enacted. Since that time the rate of adoption has increased (by approximately 77 percent) and the average time from removal to adoption has declined (by 14 months)[2]. Additionally, the Fostering Connections to Success and Increasing Adoptions Act of 2008 (P.L. 110-351) took great strides to provide additional resources to States to ensure support for increasing adoptions, but more must be done. Through the Fostering Connections Act, the Adoption Incentive Program was improved and reauthorized through fiscal year 2013.

The Fostering Connections Act revised the baselines against which adoption increases are measured, and doubled awards for increased adoptions of children age nine and older (increased to $8,000) as well as for younger children with special needs (increased to $4,000). Under the law States also have the opportunity to earn incentives for increasing their rate of adoptions (calculated by dividing the total number of adoptions by the total number of children in foster care on the last day of the fiscal year and multiplying by 100).

As you know, the Adoption Incentive program is set to expire at the end of this fiscal year and as States' overall foster care population decline, so are the number of adoption finalizations. Consistent with the national number of children in foster care decreasing so has the number of children waiting to be adopted as well (134,000 in FY2002 compared to 104,000 in FY2011). The number of children adopted from foster care each year has stayed above 51,000 since 2002. The peak was seen in fiscal year 2009, the year after the updated baseline from the Adoption Incentive Program was enacted, with 57,000 children adopted in that year. The number of children adopted in FY 2011, the last year we have data from, was 51,000 adoptions.

After the enactment of the Fostering Connections Act, all but six States and the District of Columbia have received an incentive payment in at least one year. In FY2009 all but twelve States received an incentive payment, but by FY2011 twenty-two States did not receive any incentive.[3] Since the number of children in foster care and the number of youth waiting to be adopted have declined over 20% in the past five years (this is good news), states can't continue to exceed their FY2007 baseline number of adoptions and will not be able to achieve the adoption incentives.

It is important to note that the incentive payments related to the adoption rates are only available to States if there is money left after the initial bonuses have been allocated. Despite foster care population declines, adoption rates have remained stable, which suggests that the rate of adoptions may be a greater indicator of success. Some greater priority should be given to rates of adoption, especially for older youth. For example if a State has increased their adoption rates, but not increased enough over their baseline level to achieve the per child adoption incentives, are we not providing an incentive for the rate increase achievement? The answer to this question is hard to answer, because we don't have adequate reporting on what State achievements are in each of the adoption incentive categories; we encourage this to be examined more closely.

As the Subcommittee is reviewing the reauthorization of this program, *Voice for Adoption recommends adjusting the adoption baseline to more current levels in order to ensure that the Adoption Incentives continue to be an effective approach to increasing the number of adoptions. Additionally, we request detailed reports on the number of adoptions in each category, as well as the State use of the awards. It is hard to have a clear picture of what types of increases in adoption States are receiving the bonuses for, because in recent years HHS has only reported on the total dollar amount States have earned rather than any detail of what was achieved. Additionally States are not required to report the use of the incentive dollars, so tracking use of these funds is also difficult.*

The adoption of older youth continues to be a struggle for states.

Despite the achievements we've seen in connecting waiting children with adoptive families, states still struggle to meet the needs of older youth waiting for permanent families. In a recent analysis published by the National Resource Center for Adoption, a review of data found that only 26.1 percent of all *adoptions* were of children ages 9 and older, while at the same time 40.6 percent of children *waiting* for adoption were 9 or older. This represents the lowest percentages of older youth adoptions since the enactment of ASFA in 1997. It is critical that we find ways to increase the likelihood of adoption for older youth, because otherwise we will continue to allow legal orphans to exit our nation's foster care system to unfortunate outcomes (and there has been much research dedicated to what happens to youth when they exit foster care without permanent connections). For older youth adoption, promising practices include a variety of efforts that should continue to be strengthened and taken up by states to ensure success for this population. These practices, which you will hear about in depth from my colleagues on the panel, include: youth engagement in permanency planning, smaller caseloads, intensive family finding, kinship connections and reunification efforts. To facilitate these efforts, *Voice for Adoption recommends reauthorizing the funding for the Family Connections grants,[4] which are also are set to expire at the end of this year.*

Another way to continue to promote these effective practices is to encourage States to leverage public-private partnerships to promote adoptions of children in foster care. A key provision of the Fostering Connections Act provides federal Title IV-E reimbursement for training a range of service providers and caregivers (court personnel, attorneys, guardian ad litems, court appointed special advocates, and perspective relative guardians as well as foster and adoptive parents). Funding for this provision was phased in over 5 years with full 75 percent reimbursement in fiscal year 2012 and beyond. The benefits of the training expansion of the Fostering Connections Act in promoting public private partnerships are yet to be realized. Clarity is needed from HHS on key implementation issues. *Voice for Adoption recommends that States utilize the enhanced Title IV-E training dollars toward the use of effective models that move older children out of foster care and into permanent families and we urge the Subcommittee to encourage HHS to issue guidance or further clarity identifying successful State examples of such opportunities.*

Youth who "age-out" are a vulnerable population and more must be done to secure permanency for these youth before exiting foster care.

As a system we are failing older youth. The number of youth who age out of foster care annually is more than 26,000. There is a growing trend in the percentage of emancipated youth whose parental rights have been terminated (16.3 percent in FY2011 compared to 6.1 percent in FY2000)[5]. Youth who leave foster care to live on their own face significant challenges, including homelessness and inadequate housing, limited or no postsecondary education or training, unemployment or underemployment, involvement with the criminal justice system, mental health and substance abuse challenges, and early parenthood[6]. When we take these youth away from their birth families, we have an obligation to create better circumstances for them. As a nation we must do a much better job at connecting these youth to permanency rather than emancipating them to no one and putting them on a trajectory toward poor outcomes.

An area that warrants greater examination for older youth is their designated case plan. Over the years there have been mounting and justified concerns regarding the use of APPLA as a permanency goal for children and youth in foster care. "APPLA" is: Another Planned Permanent Living Arrangement. It replaced "Long Term Foster Care" in legislation 16 years ago. It was intended to be used only when other permanency options such as reunification, adoption, and kinship or guardianship care are ruled out. Roughly 12 percent of children in care have this case goal, however some State data reflect numbers as high as 20 percent of their foster care population with this goal[7]. The APPLA term was established because far too many children were being given the permanency goal of long-term foster care and Congress made the right decision to remove that as a goal. However there is a growing concern in the field that APPLA has simply replaced long-term foster care, changing the terminology but not the outcomes for youth.

Too many youth report not being asked more than once, if at all, if they would consider being adopted and secondly youth report feeling forced down a path of independence while not fully understanding what permanency is[8]. Youth who have had parents throughout childhood and adolescence have the foundation of family while establishing greater independence. Yet, youth in foster care are asked to make the life altering decision of "choosing to want" to be adopted at the very time that developmentally they are seeking independence. Should youth refuse to consider adoption, they commonly are assigned a permanency goal of APPLA. Additionally, there is a correlation between older youth and their placement settings. Nationally, over one-third (36%) of youth in care who are age 16 and older are in group homes or institutional settings[9], where typically efforts are not made to connect them with permanent families and other caring adults.

While the APPLA case goal had good intentions and at the time was progressive in thinking, we have learned a lot about what happens to youth when they exit care alone and we have heard from the other panelists that better practices have been developed to serve this population. It is time for the federal government to revisit the use of APPLA as a permanency plan option for older youth. *Voice for Adoption recommends providing incentives to States for the reduction of youth who exit without permanent connections. Furthermore I urge this Committee to hold future hearings on this topic, to establish a national strategy to address this vulnerable population of youth.*

Post-adoption services remain a critical need, yet lack of resources legislated.

The federal government has invested millions of dollars into increasing adoptions without adequate assurances that these children and families will be safe and secure post-finalization. These services include assistance, such as: parent and youth support groups, crisis intervention, family therapy, respite care, and educational advocacy. Post-adoption services help adoptive families and children move through the predictable stages of becoming a family – working through past traumas and strengthening the well-being of all family members. A Casey Family Services report stated, "As states have increased the numbers of adoptions with legislative mandates and fiscal incentives, this push for more timely permanence for children in foster care has not been accompanied by parallel mandates or incentives for states to support families once the adoption is legalized.[10]" Parents are often faced with seeing practitioners that do not understand the dynamics of adoption and foster care – this only adds to the challenges of families who are seeking assistance to meet their children's emotional and mental health needs.

Although there has been a great deal of research on the need for quality post-adoption services, funding for such supports are not readily accessible. *Voice for Adoption recommends that a greater emphasis be placed on the access of adoption competent mental health providers and that appropriate funding streams be mandated to accomplish this goal. Specifically, we recommend that states be required to use adoption incentive bonuses for post-adoption support services for children and families.*

Federal adoption funding should be reviewed to ensure reinvestment into child welfare and adoption.

The Fostering Connections Act included a major provision that resulted in the federal government taking on a larger share of what States would otherwise be spending on adoption assistance. Before Fostering Connections, tens of thousands of children were not eligible for federal Title IV-E adoption assistance; in FY2008 states reported that just over 20 percent of adopted children who received adoption assistance received no federal support[11]. When the Congressional Budget Office scored the Fostering Connections Act they projected a $1.4 billion savings to States over ten years (and $126 million over 5 years). The federal government required States to reinvest these savings back into child welfare, including post-adoption services. Despite legislative attempts in two federal laws (the Fostering Connections Act and the Child Welfare Improvement and Innovation Act of 2011), HHS has been unable to report what types of services, if any, States are spending the savings on. Initial guidance to States following the Fostering Connections Act stated that States had the flexibility to determine and calculate the savings, but were not required to provide a specific accounting of the funds to the Department of HHS[12]. Congress enacted legislation in 2011 reiterating the expectation for an accounting of the Title IV-E adoption assistance savings. An Information Memorandum was issued to States directing agencies to "now document how savings (if any) are spent when using the applicable child eligibility criteria in the title IV-E adoption assistance program (sections 473(a)(2)(A)(ii) and (e) of the Act.[13]" Whether the funds are being reinvested into child welfare and adoption services is unknown because access to the State reports continues to be a challenge.

As States continue to accrue savings on what they would have been spending on state adoption assistance there is an even greater opportunity for an investment in making sure families are stable though the availability of post-adoption support. *Voice for Adoption believes that a percentage of the adoption funds states have saved from the federal adoption assistance de-link should be reinvested into services to support families after they adopt children from foster care, to ensure families are able to meet the ongoing needs of their children. Public reporting on the use of State reinvestment funds should also be required so State advocates have a tool to make sure funds are being reinvested.*

CONCLUSION

I would like to sincerely thank the Subcommittee for its interest in hearing perspectives for improvements to increasing adoptions from foster care. As you work to improve outcomes for children waiting to be adopted and adoptive families committed to raising children who often come with painful pasts, I hope you will take into consideration the recommendations presented before you today. In closing we appreciate the dedication of this Subcommittee; as demonstrated your work on children's issues remains a priority across party lines. We look forward to your continued efforts on behalf of children and families.

Respectfully Submitted,
Nicole Dobbins,
Executive Director
Voice for Adoption

End Notes

[1] Voice for Adoption is a coalition whose Board of Directors is composed of Adopt America Network, Adoption Exchange Association, The Adoption Exchange Inc., Child Welfare League of America, Children Awaiting Parents, Consortium for Children, Family Builders Network, Kinship Center, Lilliput Children's Services, National Adoption Center, New York Council on Adoptable Children, North American Council on Adoptable Children, Spaulding for Children-Michigan, and Three Rivers Adoption Council.

[2] National Resource Center for Adoption, A Service of the Children's Bureau & Member of the T/TA Network. The Roundtable, Volume 25: Number 2 (2012).

[3] U.S. Department of Health and Human Services, Administration for Children and Families (Aug. 2012) Adoption Incentives Earning History by State: FY 1998-FY2011. Washington, DC.

[4] Family Connections grants are for projects and integrated programs for intensive family-finding activities and family group decision-making meetings (FDGM), kinship navigator programs and residential family treatment project in supporting connections with family members to build the capacity to meet the needs of children and families.

[5] Analysis prepared by Penelope L. Maza, Ph.D. based on data from the Cornell Data Archive as of February 2013.

[6] Courtney, M.E., Dworsky, A., Hook, J., Brown, A., et al. (2011). Midwest Evaluation of the Adult Functioning of Former Foster Youth. Retrieved February 22, 2013 from: http://www.chapinhall.org/sites/default/files/Midwest%20Evaluation Report 4 10 12.pdf

[7] The case goal APPLA was enacted after AFCARS data reporting, so States still report goals of "Long Term Foster Care" or "emancipation". Establishment of one of these goals suggests that the other permanent options were ruled out. Congressional Research Service Report,

Another Planned Permanent Living Arrangement (APPLA) as a Permanency Goal for Children in Foster Care (February 2012).

[8] U.S. Senate Caucus on Foster Youth, "Call to Action," October 7, 2010. Retrieved February 21, 2013 from: http://www.finance.senate.gov/newsroom/ranking/release/?id=98aaed19-1918-41a9-a11a-d6ff11b51990

[9] Annie E. Casey, Kids Count, May 2011

[10] Casey Family Services, The Casey Center for Effective Child Welfare Practice, Promising Practices in Adoption Competent Mental Health Services (2003) Retrieved February 21, 2013 from: http://www.aecf.org/upload/publicationfiles/promising%20practices%20in%20 adoption.pdf

[11] DeVooght, K. Fletcher, M. Vaughn, B., & Cooper, H. (2012). Federal, State, and Local Spending to Address Child Abuse and Neglect in SFYS 2008 and 2010.

[12] U.S. Department of Health and Human Services. (2010). Guidance on Fostering Connections to Success and Increasing Adoptions Act of 2008. ACYF-CB-PI-10-11.

[13] U.S. Department of Health and Human Services. (2011) Child and Family Services Improvement and Innovation Act; Titles IV-B, IV-E and section 1130 of the Social Security Act; Promoting Safe and Stable Families Program; Child Welfare Services Program. ACYF-CB-IM-11-06.

In: The Adoption Incentives Program
Editors: Patrick L. Cales

ISBN: 978-1-62948-758-8
© 2014 Nova Science Publishers, Inc.

Chapter 3

TESTIMONY OF RITA L. SORONEN, PRESIDENT AND CEO, DAVE THOMAS FOUNDATION FOR ADOPTION. HEARING ON "INCREASING ADOPTIONS FROM FOSTER CARE"[*]

Good afternoon Chairman Reichert, Ranking Member Doggett and the Members of the Subcommittee. I am honored to be here and grateful for the invitation to join the hearing today.

I am Rita Soronen, president and CEO of the Dave Thomas Foundation for Adoption. For just over 20 years, the Dave Thomas Foundation for Adoption has shared the Subcommittee's quest to elevate and dramatically improve the services we provide to abused, neglected, dependent and abandoned children for whom the government has assumed temporary, but, too frequently, longterm responsibility. Created in 1992 by Dave Thomas, who was adopted, the Dave Thomas Foundation for Adoption works to dramatically increase the number of adoptions of waiting children from the United States foster care system, while providing information, resources, media awareness tools and educational materials to potential adoptive parents, individuals and organizations, at no cost to the user. Additionally, as a national nonprofit public charity, we provide grants to public and private organizations in all 50 states and the District of Columbia to results-based agencies that

---

[*] This is an edited, reformatted and augmented version of a testimony, presented February 27, 2013 before the House Committee on Ways and Means, Subcommittee on Human Resources.

aggressively and measurably move children out of foster care and into adoptive homes.

Each day, we work under the core beliefs that 1) every child deserves a safe, nurturing and permanent home, 2) no child should linger in foster care or turn 18 and leave care without the family promised when they were permanently severed from their family of origin and 3) every child, no matter the age, placement or circumstance is adoptable.

Thank you to the members of the Subcommittee for their commitment to review and assess existing policies and emerging best practices for vulnerable children and youth, with a vigilant eye on providing the most effective evidence-based services on their behalf. The Adoption Incentives program has provided critical Federal funding to help states focus on increasing older youth adoptions and making important family connections.

Although we are encouraged by an increasing national awareness about the needs of foster care youth[1] (and in particular about children waiting to be adopted), a decline in children entering care and greater numbers of children being adopted from foster care[2], we are gravely concerned about older youth waiting to be adopted.

The number of children waiting to be adopted from U.S. foster care has consistently exceeded the number of finalized adoptions in each year for which national data are available. While the overall numbers of adoptions increased in the years following the 1998 implementation of the Adoption and Safe Families Act (ASFA), the growth in adoptions of younger children has outpaced those of older children. At the same time, the numbers of older youth aging out of foster care continue to rise. In 1998, approximately 17,300 youth were emancipated from care, compared with more than 26,000 in 2011. Additionally, most recent data shows a current placement of more than 22,000 children in long-term foster care (or Planned Permanent Living Arrangement); these youth most likely will leave the system without defined permanency.[3]

Since these youth have typically spent the longest periods of time in care, the core issues of the abuse or neglect which they have experienced, combined frequently with exposure to family violence, substance abuse or lack of appropriate basic care, are exacerbated by frequent moves while in care, potential separation from siblings, multiple school or educational placements, and frequent turnover of social workers or other system contacts in their lives. The children most at risk of aging out and moving into society without the safety net of a family and a home, the youth who suffer the consequences of the government's broken promise of a family[4], are the children for whom the

Dave Thomas Foundation for Adoption has dedicated its energy, expertise and resources.

Strategies for recruiting and matching adoptive families for these children have a history of anecdotal rather than evidence-based development. Cataloging children online or through the media is common practice and supported by Federal funding, but there is scant evidence to suggest it is an effective method for effectively recruiting appropriate families for America's longest-waiting children who have individualized and often therapeutic or clinical needs. General recruitment practices through media campaigns help to make citizens more aware of the numbers of children in foster care, but cannot focus on the intense and urgent needs of children currently waiting for families.

Additionally, we know that the current ages of children in foster care waiting to be adopted, as well as their ages at the time of entry into foster care, are correlates of their likelihood of adoption. Based on analyses of national data from the Adoption and Foster Care Reporting System (AFCARS), Dr. Maza (2002) found that a waiting child's age is the most crucial characteristic affecting his or her likelihood of being adopted, and that the tipping point occurs between ages 8 and 9, after when a child is more likely to continue to wait and subsequently age out of foster care than to be adopted.[5] Her more recent analyses have shown that, despite the 1997 Adoption and Safe Families Act's intention to promote the adoption of children waiting in foster care – particularly those who are older – the share of waiting children who are over age 8 has grown in the past decade. Further, while the time children spend waiting has declined markedly, this decline occurred solely for children who entered care prior to age 8.[6] The inference that ASFA has not affected the adoption of older children highlights the critical need for innovative adoption recruitment programs.

WENDY'S WONDERFUL KIDS CHILD-FOCUSED RECRUITMENT MODEL AND MANAGEMENT

In response, the Dave Thomas Foundation for Adoption has dedicated significant private, and recently public, resources to develop, implement and grow a national model of child-focused recruitment (Wendy's Wonderful Kids) combined with long-term rigorous experimental evaluation of the model. The primary target populations for this model include older youth, sibling groups, children with mental or physical challenges, and children in placements that have typically been considered difficult adoption platforms (group homes, therapeutic placements and institutions). The program has grown from seven pilot implementation sites in 2004 to now 161 fully-funded grants at public and private adoption agencies in 49 states and the District of Columbia. Additionally, the Foundation manages the activities of the Dave Thomas Foundation for Adoption-Canada in which there are eight fully-funded sites in four provinces.

The Foundation named the grant program Wendy's Wonderful Kids to honor the significant fundraising that occurs through Wendy's restaurants across the nation, encouraging customers, employees and partners to donate to the Foundation. In turn, we dedicate funds back to the communities in which the funds are raised to support a recruiter(s) who works for children waiting to be adopted, and in particular, those children nearly everyone else has forgotten.

To date, we have served 8,789 children and found potential adoptive matches for 5,790 of these children. While 503 of the children served are currently in pre-adoptive placements, 3,406 adoptions have been finalized. Significantly, more than half of the children for whom the recruiters provided active engagement had *no* prior recruitment activities.[7] This is particularly compelling given that the average age of a child served through this program is almost 12, more than 30 percent of the children had already been in six or more placements (nine percent had experienced 10 or more placements), 50 percent had been in the system for more than four years at the point of referral into the program, 48 percent have at least one identified disability, 43 percent are referred as part of sibling groups, 20 percent reside in group homes or institutions at the time of referral, and 21 percent had already experienced failed or disrupted adoptions.

Since 2004, the Foundation has invested $53.8 million of private funding in the development and growth of Wendy's Wonderful Kids in the United States, and another $3.4 million in Wendy's Wonderful Kids in Canada. Simple math shows that given the number of adoptions finalized and dollars invested to date, each adoption has "cost" just over $16,000. Although untangling the actual costs of maintaining a child in care is a challenge, national averages point to maintenance and administrative costs of nearly $26,000 per child per year.[8]

The Wendy's Wonderful Kids child-focused recruitment concept is simple. With grant funds from the Foundation, agencies hire full-time, experienced adoption professionals who dedicate 100 percent of their days to find families for the longest-waiting children in their communities. These professionals, known as Wendy's Wonderful Kids recruiters, employ the Foundation's child-focused recruitment model and work on caseloads of children the system has forgotten, ensuring they have the time and resources to give each the attention he or she needs.

The recruiters employ aggressive practices and proven tactics focused on finding the best home for a child through the starting points of familiar circles of family, friends and neighbors, and then reaching out to the communities in which they live. The Foundation commits to one-year, renewable grants that support the salary, benefits and a portion of time of a supervisor, and ask in return that the agency commit to implementing the child-focused recruitment model, provide employment support for the recruiter hired, manage a smaller but intensive caseload of 15-20 children, and participate in monthly data reporting to the Foundation, as well as ongoing evaluation of process and results.

Critical to this relationship is the transition from passive recruitment for older and more difficult to place youth, to an aggressive and accountable method of finding families for children. The child-focused recruitment strategy is based on a specific dynamic recruitment plan tailored for the individual child and based on his or her unique circumstances, challenges, desires and needs and includes, but is not limited to, the following key components:

– *Relationship with Child:* Recruiters must meet and communicate with the child regularly to develop trust and openness. This relationship is essential to building an effective recruitment plan. Prior to the implementation of this model, adoption professionals frequently told us they never met with the children for whom they were recruiting families.

– *Case Record Review:* Recruiters must have access to, and conduct an in-depth review of, the existing case file, as well as ongoing review of relevant documents, reports and materials. An exhaustive case record review includes identification of all significant people in the child's life – past and present, including potential adoptive parents – while creating an understanding of the chronology of events, services, placements, educational and medical circumstances, and child welfare entry circumstances that the youth has experienced.

– *Network Building:* Recruiters must meet with significant adults identified in the case record review (foster parents, CASA/GALs, counselors, teachers, extended family, etc.) and maintain regular and ongoing contact. Regular contact with individuals close to and knowledgeable about the child facilitates effective recruitment and matching.

- *Child Assessment and Adoption Preparation:* Recruiters determine the child's strengths, challenges, desires, preparedness for adoption and whether the child has needs that should be addressed before moving forward with the adoption process. They must also assure that the child is prepared for adoption and during the matching process that the family is adequately prepared to meet the needs of the child.
- *Diligent Search:* Recruiters conduct a diligent search of potential adoptive families, including family members, and identified connections to additional resources and pursue aggressive follow-up with contacts, with the knowledge and approval of the child's caseworker.
- *Recruitment Plan*: Based on the file review, interviews with significant adults, assessment of and input from the child, recruiters develop and implement a comprehensive recruitment plan. The plan for each child is customized and defined by the child's needs, reviewed regularly, and updated quarterly.

The Foundation grants management and program teams provide orientation to and training of the child-focused model; communicate monthly, at a minimum, with the recruiters to discuss casework, challenges and to provide support; and make annual on-site visits with the grantees to assess fidelity to the model, review activities and meet with system representatives. Additionally, the grantee organizations provide regular financial, goal accountability and narrative reporting to the Foundation. Monthly, they must also input comprehensive data about their casework and the children on their caseloads into a database that is owned by the Foundation and managed by Washington, D.C.-based Child Trends.

CHILD-FOCUSED RECRUITMENT EVALUATION

The Wendy's Wonderful Kids strategy is to focus exhaustively on an individual child's history, experiences and needs and then make an aggressive and unrelenting effort on behalf of the child in order to find an appropriate adoptive family. At one level, the powerful individual success stories early into the program showed that the model appeared to be working; however, the

Foundation was keenly aware that no long-term evaluation of any recruitment model existed. It was critical to ensure that evidence-based activities and not an anecdotal approach drove these successful adoptions.

In 2005, the Foundation commissioned Child Trends for an unprecedented five-year evaluation of the child-focused model. *It is the most comprehensive, rigorous empirical evaluation of adoption recruitment practices completed to date in this country.* The research included both impact and process evaluations, and assessed the outcomes of randomly selected children served in 21 grantee agencies, representing 18 states, against a control group of children receiving traditional adoption recruitment methods in the same localities.

Significantly, the impact evaluation showed that children served by the child-focused Wendy's Wonderful Kids model are *1.7 times more likely to be adopted* than those not served by the program.[9] Furthermore, its impact on adoption is strongest among older youth and those with mental health disorders – groups that have traditionally waited the longest for adoption, or that are least likely to achieve adoption – those groups are up to *three times more likely to be adopted.* Additionally, the process evaluation highlighted tactics of the model that worked to encourage successful adoptions. For example, in interviews with children served, those youth who were previously opposed to adoption (and therefore those most likely to be placed on the emancipation track for aging out of care, or moved to a court-ordered Planned Permanent Living Arrangement) were significantly more likely to feel open to adoption after working with a recruiter.

One sample of a narrative sent by a recruiter in Florida exemplifies the daily success of this program:

At age 16, Dana had been in foster care for eight years, and had lived in 22 different foster care placements. He seemed resigned to figuring out how to live on his own. Dana's future changed when he was added to the caseload. I found the name of an aunt who had expressed interest in adopting Dana in the past and discovered the initial barrier to adoption had simply been inadequate housing and the agency stopped using her as a potential adoptive resource. We worked with the housing authority, helped her to complete training, finalized a second home study, and helped her to navigate the interstate child welfare rules. I am excited to report Dana was adopted yesterday, just weeks before his 18th birthday.

SCALING THE MODEL AND COST IMPLICATIONS

With the release of the national evaluation of Wendy's Wonderful Kids, the Foundation put in place a strategic blueprint to scale the program within states, while partnering with the Annie E. Casey Foundation to develop a formal child-focused recruitment curriculum, as a companion to scaling activities. Additionally, we hosted a convening of cross-discipline experts and leaders (pediatric, policy, funding, higher education, child welfare, media and public relations) to advise the Foundation on scaling, funding and policy implications of the research.[10]

In approaching our home state of Ohio, we made the case that if we were to be successful across the nation we, like our colleagues in adoption, needed to focus first in our own community. After sharing the national and local results and the evaluation findings with the leadership of the Ohio Department of Job & Family Services (ODJFS), the state committed to the resources necessary to scale Wendy's Wonderful Kids from seven existing Ohio sites to 41, serving a majority of Ohio's 88 counties and focusing on children age 9 or older and in care for two or more years. The Foundation committed to managing the increased grant sites in the way that had already proved successful in Ohio and across the nation.

In just six months and with the determined support of the administrative, program, and fiscal teams of the Ohio Department of Job & Family Services, 32 new recruiters have been hired, trained, and have growing caseloads, now at nearly 200 children. Sixteen children have already been matched with families, two are in pre-adoptive placements and a sibling group of three was just adopted last week. The director of the public agency that finalized those adoptions said:

> Through the Wendy's Wonderful Kids program, Allen County Children Services has been able to hire two highly qualified and experienced children services social workers as our specialized adoption recruiters. They work with a reduced, yet intensive caseload to achieve the goal of securing forever families for our harder-to-adopt children and sibling groups. We would not have this ability without the support of the Dave Thomas Foundation for Adoption and the Ohio Department of Job & Family Services.

Keenly aware, though, that cost implications can frequently trump best practice, we worked with the fiscal team at ODJFS to quantify the return on its investment in this program and to use the partnership as a template for other states.

For example, prior to the state's investment in scaling, the Dave Thomas Foundation for Adoption, from 2005 – 2012, invested just over $3 million in private funding in seven Ohio sites. During that time, we saw the finalization of 197 adoptions of children with an average age of 12.1 years. Given what we know about the likelihood of this population of children who are at risk for aging out of care, and calculating an annual savings of $27,480 per child (Ohio-specific figures) by getting them adopted, and while factoring in the average monthly subsidy provided to families, Wendy's Wonderful Kids saved the state of Ohio nearly $32 million.[11]

Expanding those calculations to include a current $2 million investment from the state for the scaled counties in 2013, ODJFS calculates that over three years (with additional annual commitments), and with the finalization of 650 adoptions based on historical success, the state of *Ohio will save in excess of $105 million by the end of 2015.*

Of course, these numbers represent actual hard cost savings. When we combine that with the frequently researched costs to society of not getting these children adopted, there can be no argument that both the human and the fiscal realities can no longer to be ignored.[12]

CONTINUING CHALLENGES AND HOPE

There is no more important work in this country than assuring the safety and well-being of our most vulnerable citizens – children who, through no fault of their own, are in the child welfare system waiting for permanent families. There is equally no more important promise to be kept than the one we make to our children when they have been permanently removed from their families of origin – that we will cherish their childhood, keep them safe, and find each one a family with whom they can grow and thrive. *Last year we broke that promise to 26,286 children who we negligently allowed to age out of care.*

Even with the clear human, partnership, and financial success of Wendy's Wonderful Kids, there remain challenges to address. Too many of the very adults charged with finding adoptive families for youth still believe that some children are simply too old, too damaged or too set in their ways to be adopted. Indeed, even the general population is skeptical of these children. In a Harris Interactive national survey of attitudes toward foster care adoption that the Dave Thomas Foundation for Adoption will be releasing this spring, only half of Americans believe that every child is adoptable.

At the Foundation, we continue to work to train professionals, potential adoptive parents, policymakers and the general public that no child is "unadoptable" and that we have an evidence-based model to support that belief. We have also created an award-winning national "I Am" print and broadcast media awareness campaign (*"I am not too old, I am not unlovable, I am not a troublemaker, We are not twice the burden"*) that works to eradicate the "unadoptable" notion. This month, we will release a follow-up campaign that focuses on families who have adopted older youth (*"Having a son has been an amazing life-changing experience: we met ours when he was 16)* that works to normalize the adoptions of older youth and elevate our attitudes toward their potential.

As we continue to work and scale this program across the nation, our recruiters are too often challenged by a lack of access to critical records, too few competent post-adoption services and professionals for their families, confusion and conflicting information about available health and educational resources, burdensome interstate regulations, and an incomprehensible willingness of the custodial agencies and courts to place children in permanent uncertainly, rather than moving them toward adoption.

We fervently believe that the evidence-based model of child-focused recruitment, our success at forming national public/private partnerships for children, and the promising example the state of Ohio has offered to the nation generates hope for our children and the systems that surround them. It also supports shifting resources to save scarce dollars to provide well-trained and managed workers to make life-changing efforts for youth, and refutes the practice of placing tens of thousands of children in the intolerable limbo of independence without family, Another Planned Permanent Living Arrangement without accountable review, or the purgatory of unadoptability.

Dave Thomas reminded us daily that "these children are not someone else's responsibility, they are our responsibility." And we would simply add *unadoptable is no longer acceptable.* We stand ready to continue to work with policymakers, practitioners, funders and families to assure a safe, nurturing and permanent family for every child waiting to be adopted. Not for just some of the children, but for all of the children.

Thank you for the opportunity to be with you today and for your careful review of the Adoption Incentives program and its continuing positive impact on the very children who need our best and most generous efforts.

Respectfully submitted,
Rita L. Soronen
President & CEO

End Notes

[1] Harris Interactive, National Adoption Attitudes Survey, commissioned by the Dave Thomas Foundation for Adoption, 2007.

[2] U.S. Department of Health and Human Services, Administration for Children and Families, The AFCARS Report: Preliminary FY 2011 Estimates as of July 2012 (19).

[3] Ibid.

[4] For a review, see: Wertheimer, Richard. (2002). Youth who age out of foster care: Troubled lives, troubling prospects. Child Trends Research Brief #2002-59. Retrieved from http://www.childtrends.org/Files//Child_Trends2002_12_01_RB_FosterCare.pdf September 15, 2011.

[5] Maza, P. (2002). The age factor in adoption. The Roundtable, 16(1).

[6] Maza, P. (2009). A new look at the role of ASFA and children's ages in adoption, The Roundtable, 23 (1).

[7] Malm, K., Vandivere, S., Allen, T., DeVooght, K., Ellis, R., McKlindon, A., Smollar, J., Williams, E, & Zinn, A. (2011.) Evaluation Report Summary: The Wendy's Wonderful Kids Initiative. Child Trends, Washington: DC.

[8] Zill, N., Roseman, E. (2011). Better Prospects, Lower Cost: The Case for Increasing Foster Care Adoption, Adoption Advocate No. 3, National Council for Adoption.

[9] Ibid.

[10] Gallagher & Associates (2012), 20th Anniversary Distinguished Panel of Experts: Recommendations to Scale the Wendy's Wonderful Kids Model.

[11] ODJFS, Dan Shook, Bureau of Fiscal Accountability, 12/12.

[12] The Jim Casey Youth Opportunities Initiative estimated that "the outcome differences between youth aging out of the foster and the general population is nearly $5,700,000,000 for each annual cohort of youth leaving care". Cutler Consulting (2009). Cost Avoidance: Bolstering the Economic Case for investing in Youth Aging Out of Care. Jim Casey Youth Opportunities Initiative.

In: The Adoption Incentives Program   ISBN: 978-1-62948-758-8
Editors: Patrick L. Cales   © 2014 Nova Science Publishers, Inc.

Chapter 4

TESTIMONY OF KELLY ROSATI, VICE PRESIDENT OF COMMUNITY OUTREACH, FOCUS ON THE FAMILY. HEARING ON "INCREASING ADOPTIONS FROM FOSTER CARE"[*]

Mr. Chairman and members of the committee, thank you for inviting my testimony before you this afternoon. Please allow me to introduce myself and my organization. My name is Kelly Rosati, and I am the Vice President of Community Outreach at Focus on the Family. I am also blessed, along with my husband, to have adopted our four children from the foster care system, and three of them have special needs. One of my roles at Focus on the Family is to oversee our Adoption and Orphan Care Initiative.

Focus on the Family is a donor---supported global Christian ministry that reaches about 238 million people in 130 countries. We help families thrive by providing help and resources for strengthening believers in their faith and sharing the gospel; building resilient marriages that reflect God's design; equipping parents to raise their children with a thriving faith; advocating for the preborn, orphaned and life at every stage; and engaging the culture through a biblical worldview. Visit Focus online at FocusOnTheFamily.com.

---

[*] This is an edited, reformatted and augmented version of a testimony, presented February 27, 2013 before the House Committee on Ways and Means, Subcommittee on Human Resources.

I. The Current State of the US Foster Care System

One of our nation's most intractable child---advocacy issues is the tragedy of children and youth trapped in foster care awaiting adoptive families to call their own. The children in this situation are often viewed by society as "un---adoptable" because of their age, minority status, or special need. At Focus on the Family, we reject such thinking and believe that every waiting child deserves a family. We are committed to using our voice and reach within the Christian community to recruit adoptive families for these waiting children.

We have also discovered through our national collaborative efforts with other adoption---focused organizations, including Show Hope (Christian musician Steven Curtis Chapman's organization), Hope for Orphans (a ministry of FamilyLife), and the Christian Alliance for Orphans, that despite the fact that more than 100,000 children in the United States are waiting in foster care for adoptive families[1], very few faith---based organizations and leaders of the community have focused their primary attention on recruiting adoptive families for these waiting children and youth (also considered "legal orphans" as their birth parents' rights have been terminated).

Focus on the Family's desire is to fill this significant awareness gap by calling attention to the plight of the most difficult to place and longest waiting legal orphans in the United States. Some of the reasons that these children are at increased risk are:

- Most of these children started life with abuse, neglect, or abandonment.
- Their birth parents' legal parental rights had to be terminated in order to keep them safe and provide them a chance at a happy life.
- Their only legal, permanent "parent" is the government entity (state or county) that has permanent legal custody of them.

These children live in temporary foster homes, move frequently from home to home, and have no permanency in their lives. Unless they are adopted, they will exit or "age---out" of the system at age 18 and may become adults who belong nowhere and have no permanent personal relationship connection with anyone.

In 2011, the most current year for which data is available, family courts across the country terminated more than 61,361 children's birth parents' legal parental rights, while only 50,516 children were adopted from the foster care system.[2] In fiscal year 2011, more than 26,000 children exited[3] the foster care system, many of whom face a bleak future. Of the youth who aged---out of the foster care system without permanent connections, statistics show that:

- Almost 20 percent of foster care alumni who aged out did not have a high school diploma or GED.[4]
- Only 8 percent had a postsecondary degree from either a 2--- or 4---year school.[5]
- 81 percent of male former foster youth and 59 percent of female former foster youth were arrested by age 23 or 24.[6]
- Nearly one third of girls formerly in care had been pregnant by age 18[7]
- 68 percent of girls and 42 percent of boys had been food stamp recipients. [8]
- Over half of youth who aged out of foster care experienced one or more episodes of homelessness.[9]

Without the stability and comfort of a permanent family, many youth suffer dire consequences.

II. THE EMPHASIS OF OUR INVOLVEMENT WITH CHILD WELFARE

At Focus on the Family, we believe that every child deserves a permanent family. For too long, children and youth in foster care have been overlooked and forgotten. Right now, more than 100,000 legal orphans in the U.S. foster care system are waiting for adoptive families to call their own. As we looked at the need, we found that it was not because of a lack of agency capacity or competency that these children and youth are waiting. Rather, a lack of adoptive families causes them to wait. Therefore, our primary objective is to raise awareness of and recruit families for waiting kids in foster care.

The combination of our deeply held convictions coupled with the fact that there are more than 300,000 churches in the United States leads us to believe that by mobilizing the thousands of faith communities around the country, we will see a reduction in the number of waiting children throughout our foster care system. In some communities, this has already proven true.

In order to accomplish this, we launched *Wait No More: Finding Families for Waiting Kids* events. We collaborate with government officials (state and county), adoption agencies, church leaders and ministry partners to host half--day events. Through the event and robust, targeted media campaigns, *Wait No More* is highlighting the urgent need for adoptive parents.

At the *Wait No More* event, attendees have the opportunity to hear different perspectives on adoption from foster care from adoptive parents, adopted youth, siblings, and social workers. We do not sugarcoat the difficulties inherent in the process.

To the contrary, we spend time explaining the common behavioral challenges, the reasons behind such challenges, and strategies for successful child and family outcomes.

In addition, on the day of the event, adoption agencies and support ministries are on site to answer questions and help families take the next step in the process. Most importantly, families have the opportunity to start the process of adoption from foster care before they leave the event.

Families are able to choose an agency they prefer to work with, and those who do not choose an agency on that day are matched with agencies based on criteria such as agency service area and capacity.

We coordinate with the agencies after the event regarding those families, and they typically receive a call from the agency within 3 business days of the event.

III. PROGRAM OUTCOMES

To date, through 15 events and three online campaigns, more than 2,100 families have started the process of adoption from foster care through the collaborative efforts of *Wait No More*. Additional events are planned around the country in the hopes that children and youth in foster care will *Wait No More* for the forever families they deserve.

Here in Colorado, we have invested heavily in recruitment efforts in order to see the number of waiting kids reduced. In 2008 when we hosted our first event, more than 800 children and youth were awaiting permanent families. As a result of both the *Wait No More* efforts and the ongoing work of excellent agencies and ministries throughout the state, that number is down to about 270 waiting kids. (To read an article on the reduction in the number of waiting kids in Colorado, please see Appendix A.)

Any group working independently cannot achieve results such as these. However, through greater collaboration between child welfare, licensed child placing agencies, and churches, the results are multiplied. Through 15 events to date in twelve different states, more than 8,300 people have attended an event representing 4,500 families and 2,100 churches. As stated previously, more than 2,100 families have started the process of adoption from foster care, which is slightly more than 40 percent of families in attendance.

In May of 2011, the Gillett family attended a Wait No More event in Michigan. Here is their story:

> We have now adopted twin boys. The adoption was finalized on June 20, 2012, just five days before their 16th birthdays. They had been in the system about four years and had given up hope. We have had many struggles along the way, but God in his grace sees us through the rough roads we've traveled. After 12 years of being empty nesters, we have had to make big adjustments. It's been both the hardest and the most rewarding thing we've ever done. I wish more people would adopt a child who only wants to know someone cares! I love our boys! We are blessed!

Similarly, the Savoca family attended an event in Florida:

> We considered all the different ways to adopt and chose adoption from foster care primarily because of our church adoption ministry and *Wait No More*. After attending the *Wait No More* conference in Fort Lauderdale, Florida and hearing Tiffany Jorgenson's story about being adopted at the age of 11, we felt led to consider adopting an older child and prayed about it for several months. We eventually connected with 10--year---old Carlos who liked pizza and enjoyed quoting movie lines. We continued to pray for God's guidance and wisdom, even as we encountered some difficult setbacks. The transition period was long and often difficult but we are encouraged because we see him blossoming into a wonderful young man. We are also rejoicing because Carlos recently accepted the Lord as his Savior! We are very blessed with Carlos and know the Lord is going to do mighty things in our son's life!

Stories such as these are the impetus behind the work that we do. Included in Appendix B is a brief overview of the *Wait No More* event hosted in September 2011 at Overlake Christian Church in Washington State.

IV. CRUCIAL FACTORS CONTRIBUTING TO THE SUCCESS OF *WAIT NO MORE*

When considering in what locations we will host events, several criteria are used to help determine the feasibility of a successful event in a given area. Criteria include:

- Support from local county and/or state government
- Private and/or public child placing organizations with state contracts to place children and the capacity to handle additional families
- Area churches willing to serve as host as well as additional churches willing to promote the event within their congregations
- Funding secured through Focus on the Family

County and/or State Government Support

Having done events in 12 different states, we have yet to encounter a negative reaction from the state or county government. While they may have initial concerns about how the event will work, how families will be served, and how much capacity their staff and contracted partners have, we have been able to overcome those questions and work collaboratively towards a successful event. We have found state commissioners, directors, and caseworkers overall enthusiastic about additional efforts to find families for waiting kids. Our goal is simply to enhance the success of the work being done day in and day out.

Private and/or Public Child Placing Agency Capacity

While we know families will more than likely hit some roadblocks throughout the process of adoption, our hope is that this first step in starting the process will not be the first roadblock. With an average of 122 families starting the process at each event, it is important to ensure that public and private agencies combine to have enough capacity to handle the influx of families. This has, at times, prevented us from moving forward in certain locations. Recruiting adoptive families for waiting kids in foster care is a difficult endeavor. We want to do all we can to make the process as smooth as it should be. On the other hand, we discuss the importance of the process – with all its frustrations – in preparing families for the monumental task of welcoming home a waiting child or youth.

Church Involvement

The selection of the right host church can be complex. It is important to have a venue large enough to handle the event, positive name recognition, easy access for attendees unfamiliar with the area, and support from senior church leadership. It is also crucial to engage other local pastors and lay leaders in promotion of the event.

Marketing

The bulk of our costs are spent marketing the event, primarily to our Focus on the Family constituency. In order to best leverage Focus on the Family's influence, we focus our efforts through faith---based media channels including traditional radio, print and social media. We also distribute church---based promotional materials including video, bulletin inserts, flyers, and posters. We host a lunch six to eight weeks before the Wait No More event with pastors and faith---based leaders in order to cast the vision for the event, provide materials, and secure promotion commitments.

Event Funding

One of the first questions of concern to child welfare officials, private agencies, and other ministries is the cost to implement an event like this. Each *Wait No More* event is completely underwritten by the generosity of Focus on the Family donors. No agency or ministry is charged to participate nor is any family charged to attend. However, we do realize there are some costs associated with licensing families or pursuing adoption that are the responsibility of each party.

Once a determination can be made on the strength of the above criteria, we move forward with collaborative planning and marketing of the event.

V. OUTSIDE ENDORSEMENTS FOR WAIT NO MORE

Since the inception of *Wait No More*, many have commented on the effectiveness of the program. Below are a few things of note:

- Recognition at the White House observance of National Adoption Month in Washington, D.C. on November 28, 2011
- The Congressional Coalition on Adoption Institute (CCAI) briefing in May 2010 highlighted successful models of foster and adoptive parent recruitment for federal legislators and staff
- Recognition by the National Council for Adoption in "Engaging the Private Sector to Increase Positive Permanency Outcomes for Children in Foster Care" in September 2011
- Participation in a private gathering with leading adoption advocate US Senator Mary Landrieu in December 2011
- Invitation to the White House Office of Faith---Based and Community Initiatives Community forum in Denver in July 2011
- From the Denver Post: "It was phenomenal. It's never happened before that we had faith---based groups, county governments, the state and other agencies in one place at one time," [Dr. Sharen] Ford said. "People Care about Colorado's kids."[10]
- From the Wall Street Journal: "Yet it is the efforts of Focus on the Family...that have produced the most striking results so far. The group announced...that it would be devoting a considerable amount of its resources to a new initiative called Wait No More."[11]
- The Heritage Foundation: "Wait No More has delivered unprecedented rates of success in finding families for waiting children...States should enthusiastically pursue opportunities for parent recruitment through faith---based communities."[12]

Thank you for your time today and for considering reauthorizing the Adoption Incentives Program. Please let us know if we can be of further assistance.

Kelly Rosati
Vice President,
Community Outreach Focus on the Family

APPENDIX A. ADOPTION INITIATIVE HALVES NUMBERS OF KIDS NEEDING FAMILIES

By Electa Draper
The Denver Post
http://www.denverpost.com/news/ci_14516591

The number of Colorado children in foster care awaiting permanent adoption has been cut in half by a partnership between churches and government that places parentless kids in "forever homes."

When the Colorado Springs---based ministry Focus on the Family began spearheading the "Wait No More" adoption initiative in November 2008, the state had 8,000 children in foster care. That number included almost 800 children who were eligible for adoption because their parents had lost parental rights after the state found serious and repetitive neglect and abuse in their families.

In early 2010, only 365 children eligible for adoption remain in foster care, said Sharen Ford, manager of permanency services for the Colorado Department of Human Services.

The success of the initiative has surprised even its many partners — the state, nine counties, New Life Church in Colorado Springs, and dozens of other churches and private agencies. Ford called the results "phenomenal."

Last year alone, more than 1,000 adoptions became final, Ford said. Because children constantly enter and leave the system, the numbers are always in flux, but by the end of 2009, 6,287 were in foster care.

"I'm stunned by the number of kids we've moved off the waiting list," Focus on the Family president and chief executive Jim Daly said. "I was one of those kids — a kid that doesn't have a mom and dad. I was never adopted, but I was very appreciative of the people who came along to mentor me."

Daly said orphan care is a core mission of Christianity.

"If my Bible math is right, God reminds us 47 times to take care of widows and orphans," Daly said. "This country has something like 300,000 churches and 130,000 orphans. The math is pretty simple."

The average age of a waiting child in Colorado is 11 to 12.

"We Talk Kids"

Daly said Ford and the state Human Services staff impressed him. "They care so much about the kids."

For her part, Ford said she considers it a remarkable public---private relationship.

"We don't talk religion. We don't talk politics," she said. "We talk kids."

Tiffany Beal, now a 20---year---old college senior in Colorado Springs, was in foster care for about three years before her adoption at age 11. She urges people to go out on a limb and adopt — because it's the best thing they can do for a child.

"The most amazing part of being adopted was that no matter what, I always had a home. I had someone to call Mom and Dad," Beal said. "Even at 3, my little brother knew he wasn't home in foster care. He kept asking me, 'When are we going to go home?' "

Prospective parents can hear about the challenges and rewards of adoption and then — if they choose — begin the long adoption process at "Wait No More" events.

Focus held such an event in Colorado Springs in November 2008. At one in October in Loveland, 50 families took the first steps to adopt children. The next is scheduled for September in Denver, where there are currently 116 children available for adoption.

Other participating counties are Adams, Arapahoe, Broomfield, Boulder, Larimer, El Paso, Jefferson and Pueblo.

Ford said the screening for adoptive families is extensive. Social workers attempt to match the needs of children — many of whom have experienced a great deal in their short lives — to families' capabilities. But the process is also inclusive, she says.

Colorado law allows for adoptive families to be two---parent, single---parent, older or otherwise nontraditional, including gay households.

"We try to screen people in," Ford said. "Everybody wants to have a forever home. And there are no such things as perfect families. We need families who are flexible — who have humor."

Room for Four More

Bill, whose last name is being withheld to ensure his family's safety, last year adopted four siblings between the ages of 3 and 10. He and his wife already had four children.

His biggest anxiety was the sheer number of unknowns, from the kids' favorite foods to potential emotional triggers from past traumas.

"The most amazing thing is that they've been in our home less than a year, but it feels like it's been a lot longer — in a good way," Bill said, laughing. "From that first weekend, it felt as if it was meant to be. But that first weekend, there was a lot of explaining."

At Focus, the initiative is a national effort, said Kelly Rosati, senior director of the ministry's Sanctity of Life division.

In addition to the two adoption events in Colorado, Focus has held such meet---ups in St. Louis, Los Angeles and Fort Lauderdale, Fla. Of those attending, 830 families initiated the adoption process at the events. About 750 different churches have been involved.

"We are not giving up or stopping until every waiting child in Colorado has the family it deserves," Rosati said.

Electa Draper: 303---954---1276 or edraper@denverpost.com.

Find Out More

Don't want to wait until the next adoption event?
Visit icareaboutorphans.org to learn about adopting kids from foster care.

APPENDIX B. FINDING FAMILIES FOR WASHINGTON'S WAITING KIDS RESULTS OVERVIEW

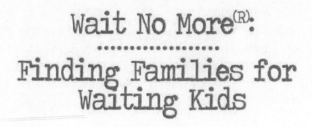

- Hosted Wait No More at Overlake Christian Church on Saturday, September 24, 2011
- Approximately 630 people attended
- Those people represented more than 345 different families
- Of those, 111 families initiated the process of adoption from foster care at the event; this represents 32.0% of families in attendance
- 15 agencies and ministries were on site to answer participants' questions and help them start the process of adoption from foster care including:
  - A Family for Every Child Heart Gallery
  - Antioch Adoptions
  - Bethany Christian Services
  - City Ministries
  - Department of Social and Health Services of Washington
  - Olive Crest
  - Overlake Christian Church
  - Youth for Christ
- More than 160 different churches were represented at *Wait No More*
- All participating families received complimentary copies of Focus on the Family resources: *Handbook on Thriving as an Adoptive Family, Wait No More: One Family's Amazing Adoption Journey,* and "Wrapping Around Adoptive Families"

End Notes

[1] AFCARS Report #19, July 2012, page 1. http://www.acf.hhs.gov/sites/default/files/cb/ afcars report19.pdf

[2] AFCARS Report #19, July 2012, page 1. http://www.acf.hhs.gov/sites/default/files/ cb/afcars report19.pdf

[3] AFCARS Report #19, July 2012, page 3. http://www.acf.hhs.gov/sites/default/files/cb/ afcars report19.pdf

[4] Mark Courtney, Amy Dworsky, Gretchen Cusick, Judy Havlicek, Alfred Perez, Tom Keller, "Midwest Evaluation of the Adult Functioning of Former Foster Youth: Outcomes at Age 21." Chapin Hall Center for Children, University of Chicago, (December 2007): 20.

[5] Ibid., 20.

[6] Ibid., 93.

[7] Ibid., 74.

[8] Ibid., 43-44.

[9] Peter Pecora, Ronald Kessler, Jason Williams, Kirk O'Brien, Chris Downs, Diana English, James White, Eva Hiripi, Catherine White, Tamera Wiggins, & Kate Holmes, "Improving Foster Family Care: Findings from the Northwest Foster Care Alumni Study." Casey Family Programs, (2005).

[10] "Adoption effort gets 'phenomenal' results," The Denver Post, November 2008. http://www.denverpost.com/breakingnews/ci 11075305

[11] "Adoption season for evangelicals," The Wall Street Journal, September 2010. http://online.wsj.com/article/SB10001424052748703743504575494263102089970.html

[12] "Foster Care: Safety Net or Trap Door?" The Heritage Foundation, Thomas C. Atwood, pg. 14, March 2011.

In: The Adoption Incentives Program   ISBN: 978-1-62948-758-8
Editors: Patrick L. Cales   © 2014 Nova Science Publishers, Inc.

Chapter 5

TESTIMONY OF PAT O'BRIEN, EXECUTIVE DIRECTOR, YOU GOTTA BELIEVE! THE OLDER CHILD ADOPTION & PERMANENCY MOVEMENT, INC. HEARING ON "INCREASING ADOPTIONS FROM FOSTER CARE"[*]

Hi there! I am Pat O'Brien, Founder and Current Executive Director of You Gotta Believe! The Older Child Adoption & Permanency Movement, Inc an organization that first and foremost considers itself a homelessness prevention program. The way we prevent homelessness is to find permanent parents for teens and young adults before they are discharged from the foster care system to no one but themselves.

I want to thank you so much for allowing me to testify on behalf of You Gotta Believe before the Human Resources Subcommittee of the Committee on Ways and Means as you are addressing the very important topic of increasing adoptions from foster care through the Adoption Incentives program.

When I started You Gotta Believe back in 1995 I noticed an interesting statistic when homeless populations were surveyed. In every survey I looked at, over half the homeless reported having grown up in foster care as youth.

---

[*] This is an edited, reformatted and augmented version of a testimony, presented February 27, 2013 before the House Committee on Ways and Means, Subcommittee on Human Resources.

They had actually come into our system first and foremost for their own safety and wellbeing only to be placed in harm's way when they were discharged from the very same system. I believe this sad result is the direct product of two primary barriers.

TWO PRIMARY BARRIERS

The first barrier is simple: Lack of belief that we can find permanent parents for teens and young adults as they are aging out of foster care. This "lack ofÆ belief keeps laws from being created that would mandate concurrent planning at the exit end of the system. My over 25 years of experience has taught me that our child welfare system must never stop recruiting permanent parents for children of any age that are at risk of aging out to our nation's streets.

And this leads to *the second barrier:* A Child Welfare Permanency Planning Goal call: Some Other Planned Permanent Living Arrangement Which May Include a Residential Education Program (SOPPLAWMI- A-REP.) Many in our field refer to this permanency planning goal as Another Planned Permanent Living Arrangement or simply APPLA.

APPLA is focused on preparing youth for adulthood. APPLA focuses on skills development and teaching youngsters the important skills to survive in the world on their own. And though skills development and preparing for adulthood is very important, there are still very few, if any, youth in the general population (including yours and my children over the age of 21) making it on their own without the help of their parents.

For example, did you know that the overwhelming majority of 22 year old college graduates who comes from fairly well-off one or two-parent families return home to their parents after they graduate from college with a four year bachelor's degree?

Also, did you know that according to the US Census the average age a youth leaves home in the United States of America is 26?

But we, as a child welfare system, are putting youth between the ages of 18 and 21 in harm's way without even trying to get them permanent parents before they are discharged from our foster care system because there is no law that mandates even the effort.

SO HOW DO WE FIND PERMANENT PARENTS FOR AGING OUT YOUTH

If our law makers ever decide to have concurrent planning at the exit end of the system whereby we not only prepare youth for adulthood by teaching them independent living skills, but we also simultaneously mandate the recruitment of permanent parents for them as well, *You Gotta Believe* can be very helpful in showing the world how relatively easy it is to find those permanent parents for our aging out youth. *You Gotta Believe* utilizes a three prong approach to finding lifetime parents for aging out youth that we call our *Saving F.A.C.E {Friends, Acquaintances, and Community Education.} Approach to Finding Permanent Parents for Youth --- Barring No One.*

1) The Friend's Approach

You see, once we believe that a permanent parent must be found for every youth before they age out of the foster care system, and we legally mandate that effort, the first place we look for this permanent parent is talking to the constructive adults who are already in an individual youth's life. People such as:

Social Workers; Employers and co-worker; Facebook Friends ;
Coaches or Other Extracurricular people;
Former babysitters; Former Foster Parents and/or former foster parents
neighbors, friends, and family
members; Unexplored Maternal and/or Paternal relatives; People re-met
at family Funerals; Child Care Staff;
Administrative Staff; School Teachers & Other School Personnel;
Therapists; Volunteers & Mentor;, AWOL
Resources; God Parents; and parents of best friends, co-workers, &
teammates (This is a just a partial list of
lifetime parents we have found and adoptive placements we have made
over the years at You Gotta Believe!)

And when we identify someone known to the youth we ask that person to take a 10 week learning and preparation experience (we call our learning experience A-OKAY or Adopting Older Kids And Youth) to see if making a lifetime commitment to this youth they so care about is something that they can do. Our statistics and research show this is the single most effective way to recruit a lifetime parent for a youth aging out of care. During a four year period under a Federal Demonstration grant it took nearly 1,000 prospective applicants from the general public to walk through our doors for an orientation to get 37 youth a life time parent. During that same four year period it only took 154 prospective applicants to walk through our doors who knew a teen to get 83 youth placed into a lifetime family. This approach is a simple highly efficient means of recruiting permanent parents that lead to the creation of permanent adoptive families for youth aging out between ages 18 and 21.

2) The Acquaintances Approach

There are many youth in the system where it is believed by the people around them that they have no constructive adults in their lives that one can reach out to. For these youth we set up opportunities for them to share the same time and space with our prospective and certified families. We do this by bringing youth into our A-OKAY parent preparation classes as consultants to teach our prospective families what it is like to be a teen growing up in foster care system. Many families who came forward having no interest in adopting teens had decided that a teen on our panel was someone that they could adopt. Dozens and dozens of youth have been placed as a direct result of sharing the same time and space and becoming acquaintances with the prospective and certified families who were taking our A-OKAY classes. This is the second best way we have found to find permanent parents for the oldest of the older youth in care.

3) The Community Education Approach

Years ago our organization realized that we were having little success trying to sell what we were doing to the general public in 15 or 30 second sound bites. That is why we created our own media, both TV and radio. One half hour at a time dedicated to the need to find permanent parents for teens and young adults about to be discharged from the foster care system. These broadcasts introduced the general public to the teens in need of families and the permanent parents who adopted the teens. In addition we had special guests who served both populations talking about the special needs of both populations.

We do a cable access program that anyone can watch while it live-streams in Brooklyn, New York, where our main office is. This broadcast serves a local purpose of recruiting local parents and a more global purpose by introducing and inspiring the rest of the world by meeting the wonderful youth who need homes and the parents who adopt them in one half hour of thoughtful interviews and conversations. In addition, we do a live radio broadcast every Sunday evening which is also live streamed on the internet and archived on a website. All the links to access these important broadcasts are included in my written statement.

Our Community Education efforts earned us the Adoption Excellence Award in 2007 from the Department of Health and Human Services in the category of *Media/Public Awareness of Adoption From Foster Care.*

To access our Television program website: http://bricartsmedia. org/ community-media/bcat-tv-network *And then click on Channel 2 every and any Thursday at 12 noon and again at 8pm Eastern Time.*

To access our radio program website: www.am1240wgbb.com every Sunday evening from 8-8:30pm Eastern Time. Should you miss the broadcast it will be archived by the end of the following week and can be listen to at www.adoptingteensandtweens.com Should you be in the New York City area you can listen on the radio on 1240 on the AM dial if you are in Nassau County, Western Suffolk County, most parts of Queens, many parts of Brooklyn, and the New Jersey Shore.

WHERE SHOULD ADOPTION INCENTIVES AWARDS BE RE-INVESTED?

There are two equally important areas where re-investing adoption incentive funds would be extraordinary useful as we place older youth with permanent parents to create life time families through adoption.

The first is funding to continue efforts to recruit the very permanent parents that we know are out there for each and every youth. Re-investing these incentive dollars to utilize the three prong strategies noted above would be an impactful way to get more youth into permanent families *before* their discharge from the system. Parents and families are the foundation and springboard to every child's future. Parents and families give every youth access to the village we so often talk about needing to raise children. It sure does take a village to raise a child *but only if* that child has a parent in that village to provide the foundation he or she needs. This is equally true for the

18, 19, 20, or 21 year olds as it would be for an infant, toddler or latency age child. Secondly, we must support families after their youth move in. Almost all the youth at the age range we place have had serious trauma in their lives. We prepare parents for what to expect, but we must also be there to support them during their hard times after their new sons and daughters move in. Funds should be reinvested to help these families maintain their commitments during the inevitable episodes and outbreaks that surface due to each youth's individual trauma. The more we support these newly created families, the stronger these families will remain. If we can provide these two basic adoption services, then each youth will have what the child welfare system promised them when they first came into foster care: and that promise was a home that provides safety, the opportunity for well-being, and a permanent parent and family who will be there for them long after their years in foster care are over.

I want to thank Chairman Rep. Dave Reichert and Ranking member Rep. Lloyd Doggett and the rest of the sub-committee on Human Resources for giving me the opportunity to represent *You Gotta Believe! The Older Child Adoption & Permanency Movement, Inc* at today's hearing. Some readings I would recommend include the following (feel free to e-mail at ygbpat@msn.com if you would like for me to e-mail any of these papers or articles to you):

Avery, Rosemary J., An Examination of Theory and Promising Practice for Achieving Permanency for Teens *Before* They Age Out of Foster Care, *Children & Youth Services Review* 32 (2010) pgs. 399-408.

O'Brien, Patrick, When You Take the P.A.R.E.N.T. Out of PERMANENT You re Left With M.(ostly) N.(ot) E.(nough) Paper written for a workshop presented at a North American Council on Adoptable Children Conference.

O'Brien, Patrick, Youth Homelessness and the Lack of Adoptive and Other Permanent Parental Planning For Teens In Foster Care: Preventing Homelessness Through Parenting. Paper written for a workshop presented at a North American Council on Adoptable Children Conference.

O'Brien, Patrick Unconditional Commitment: The Only Love That Matters to Teens An Article written and published in *Fostering Families Today* and a variety of other publications and newsletters.

Respectfully Submitted by, Pat O'Brien, MS, LMSW
Founder & Executive Director
You Gotta Believe! The Older Child Adoption
& Permanency Movement, Inc

INDEX